clotnasseen!

IRISH COARSE FISHING

The River Inny near Lough Derravaragh, County Westmeath

Irish Coarse Fishing

JAMES WILLIAMS

ADAM & CHARLES BLACK · LONDON

FIRST PUBLISHED 1968
BY A. AND C. BLACK LTD.
4, 5 AND 6 SOHO SQUARE LONDON W.I

SBN 7136 0574 X

PRINTED IN GREAT BRITAIN BY
BILLING & SONS LTD., GUILDFORD AND LONDON

CONTENTS

ILLUSTRATIONS

ACKNOWLEDGMENTS

I am indebted to J. W. Jones, D.Sc., Ph.D., senior lecturer in Zoology at Liverpool University, for his assistance with the typescript, and to Peter H. Tombleson, F.Z.S., Secretary of the National Anglers' Council, for his valuable help on several matters.

I am most grateful to Desmond Brennan, Organising Controller of the Irish Inland Fisheries Trust Incorporated, for information provided.

To both the Irish Tourist Board (Bord Failte Eireann) and the Northern Ireland Tourist Board I tender thanks for the use of their excellent photographs.

My grateful thanks are also due to hosts and local angling officials who have patiently answered many questions and otherwise tended to my needs.

I cannot conclude without paying tribute to the late C. E. R. (Toby) Sinclair, M.A., who as Coarse Fishing Adviser to the aforesaid Trust, gave assistance to many angling visitors, none the least myself, during my travels in Ireland.

I HAVE BEEN a fortunate angler. Long before Irish coarse fishing attained the popularity it enjoys today, I was introduced to the loughs and rivers of Ireland, where I experienced the pleasure of using the spinner and the white maggot in waters which had rarely, if ever, seen either form of bait.

Today there are still waters which have only occasionally witnessed the presence of coarse fishermen, and for many years to come, anglers will be able to enjoy unspoilt fishing and pursue the sport they have decided to take up, in the restful and relaxing Irish countryside.

The attitude towards coarse fishing has changed much since I first set foot in Ireland. I have had the privilege of watching the gradual growth of various fishing centres, to which an ever increasing number of angling visitors have come as year followed year. Irish coarse fishing is now an industry of national importance, and this book deals with its growth and of the experiences of one who has appreciated and observed its development.

Elementary instructions on, and reference to the basic principles of coarse fishing are outside the scope of this book, much as I am aware that a certain number of people who visit Ireland are still serving, or indeed, have not commenced to serve their angling apprenticeship. Various recommended books exist which readily deal with these matters, and the knowledge gained therefrom can be put to good use by the intending angler, when he finds himself in Ireland standing before one of its loughs or rivers.

What I have endeavoured to do is to introduce the reader to Ireland generally, to give some indication of the various types of water there, to describe the development of Irish coarse fishing, the peculiarities and habits of its coarse fish, and lastly, to present to the reader a cross-section of incidents and events

I have experienced, from which I hope he will be able to form a reasonable opinion of Ireland and of its coarse fishing.

As a youth I paid frequent visits to the country residence of an uncle, where, no more than a meadow or two from the end of his land, flowed the Welsh Dee, in which many dace, roach, gudgeon and perch, and in the quieter stretches bream, could be found. An elder cousin of mine lived in the district and he would call for me at an early hour. If we were not to visit the river, we would race away in his sports car to a mere, or lake or pond containing rudd, perch and pike and sometimes tench and carp, and inevitably eels.

The war came and I went to live with my uncle and at every opportunity I would assemble my tackle and make my way across the countryside, fishing almost where I wished and rarely encountering another being.

The war ended and another of my angling cousins invited me to accompany him to Ireland. He had relations in Dublin, Carrick-on-Shannon, by the River Slaney and on the very shores of Lough Conn itself. I could extend this list, but the very mention of these places, I am sure, conjures up sufficient thoughts on salmon, trout and pike fishing and angling for bream and rudd, for one to realise how fortunate I was to have such a relation as an ardent angling companion.

Since that memorable day when I first set foot in the capital of the Republic, I have travelled extensively in Ireland and had my share of angling fortunes and experiences. Verily I have seen 2 lb. rudd safely in the net, a 25 lb. pike played out, and witnessed those rare moments when 8 lb. bream and even larger specimens were close to hand.

A recent calculation I made showed me that I had spent several hundred days in Ireland, and on looking back I recall that few of them have been spent entirely away from lough shore or river bank, and very few nights have passed without the presence of some form of social activity. One must sleep, of course, but it is always difficult to leave a party, and "adieus" to hosts and companions always seem to be made with a certain reluctance. Social evenings are an important part of one's stay in Ireland, for not only do they offer a contrasting form of pleasure from angling but they also help one to get to know the Irish people, and in addition, something of the way of life and normal angling practices can be learned from anglers who hail from all over Britain.

Ireland is a country steeped in history; it is also a land of contrasting beauty. I can no more resist stealing away from the river, and meditating within the walls of a once formidable castle, than I can resist exploring the narrow lanes of Cavan, or wandering about the hills of Leitrim, or viewing the superb coast line of Waterford, or simply tarrying a while at some quiet spot and discovering how true the saying is, that in Ireland time can really stand still.

Cyril Smith in the introduction to his short but excellent book, *Coarse Fishing Today*, states that "the progressive, modern, coarse fisherman puts the study of fish and water conditions first, and then improvises a method and style to suit just those conditions and no others". The angler of these modern times can approach the water with a beautifully designed rod, superior line and a fixed-spool reel with a high quality action, but all too often he cannot put his thoughts and ideas into practice because of crowded banks or the existence of some form of restrictive angling legislation.

It is doubtful whether such restrictions are likely to thwart the angler who seeks coarse fish in Eire or Northern Ireland, for many years to come.

Principal coarse fishing centres of Ireland

A good catch of roach, taken from the Fairy Water, Omagh

Chapter One

THE GENERAL OUTLOOK

OF ALL THE PHRASES which have been used to describe Ireland as a coarse fishing resort, "The Angler's Paradise" is by far the most popular. It is a commonplace phrase and one has the right to ask whether there is really any justification for it being used so freely in connection with the fishing of that country. What are the facts? Ireland is a country favoured with a multitude of rivers and loughs. At least a dozen of these rivers provide coarse fishing of the highest standard, and the number of loughs containing coarse fish runs into several hundred. Ireland has so much good salmon and trout fishing, that coarse fishing, until more recent years, has been pursued on a rather limited scale. Since 1945 however, the outlook has changed; the country has welcomed an ever-increasing number of coarse fishermen to its shores, and many excellent catches have been recorded from its infrequently fished waters.

There are only four species of coarse fish found in any great number in Ireland, but they are distributed in all but a few well-defined areas which are principally in the north-western and south-western parts of the country. These fish are the perch, pike, rudd, and common bream. Dace inhabit but one waterway, and roach have only a slightly better distribution. There are certain rivers and loughs in which tench exist, but the full extent of their distribution is still not known. Other coarse fish, as for example carp and gudgeon, are present in Ireland but they are neither numerous nor widespread. Thus, generally the visitor will find himself fishing for one or more of the four most common species of fish. Perch, although numerous, are generally small in size. They will often keep the angler

B

active and amused by their bold biting antics, but will not
especially satisfy him. Rudd, however, do grow to goodly
proportions and there are no more attractive fish in Ireland
when their weight is around the 1 lb. mark. They fight well and
the location of a shoal of large rudd can provide the angler
with much good fishing. Bream too, grow large, and as with
the rudd many specimen fish swim in Irish waters. They are
exceedingly strong fighters, and it is quite usual for the angler
to find himself taking bream of a good average weight. Pike,
too, grow to a large size, but the increase in the popularity of
pike fishing in Ireland, especially in the past decade, together
with the removal of many of them to benefit other forms of
angling, has reduced their numbers somewhat. However, when
one is fishing pike waters, of which there are many in Ireland,
there is always an outside chance of landing a large fish. To
complete the overall picture I would mention that if an angler
finds himself in an area where tench, dace or roach exist, the
average size of these fish should not cause disappointment.

To sum up, although the angler is somewhat restricted in the
actual number of species of fish he can catch, the average
weight of these fish provides generous compensation for the
loss in variety. The capture of record fish is an act which has
always been reserved for the fortunate few, and while one must
not always expect to experience remarkable fishing, one always
has an excellent chance of enjoying coarse fishing of a high
standard. To some there will in addition be the novelty of, say,
river fishing for rudd and pike. There is also the rare privilege
of being able to wander at random and to select one's swim
at one's leisure, for there is freedom in Ireland and a limitless
amount of water to explore.

The more common types of hookbait and groundbait can
usually be procured locally, and there is normally at least one
tackle shop in each district. The prudent angler will, however,
take with him a good supply of both tackle and bait, for should
he require to supplement his stock of either item, it is obvious
that needs cannot always be catered for. Fishing districts

should be carefully chosen. Brochures on every recognised angling centre are available from official sources, and also Ordnance Survey Maps, and thus no difficulties should arise concerning the accessibility of water or in connection with the type of angling one wishes to pursue.

I must mention that although much of the coarse fishing in Eire is free, and all legitimate forms of angling are allowed, certain loughs and rivers are controlled by the Inland Fisheries Trust Incorporated. Only members of the Trust can fish such waters, and at the time of writing the annual fee is 10s. This organisation performs a multitude of tasks for the general benefit of Irish fishing, and members receive periodically reports on its latest activities, and much interesting information on such subjects as stocking, the capture of specimen fish, and the like.

In Northern Ireland it is necessary to obtain a licence before angling for coarse fish in certain districts, and it is therefore advisable to make enquiries before commencing to fish.

To complete the general picture, it is necessary to refer to the physical and climatic conditions of Ireland, and also to comment on the actual existence and locations of coarse fish.

The hills and mountains of Ireland are, for the most part, situated in the coastal regions of the country, and much of its trout and salmon fishing is to be found in such areas, where many of its rivers and streams flow swiftly down to the sea, and provide game fishing of the highest quality. The coarse fishing districts are thus mainly found in what is known as the Central Plain of Ireland, through which the River Shannon flows and where, in the northern counties of the Republic, so many of its loughs are situated.

· The Central Plain which covers an appreciable part of Ireland, is of limestone, often lying beneath bog. It is an area of contrasting features and some of its lakeland scenery is as magnificent as any found elsewhere in Ireland. One associates limestone with two important aspects, the first being the presence of much natural food, which is so essential in the development of good quality fish. The alkaline content of the waters on the limestone differs from one to another, but is of no material consequence, as is borne out by the fine specimen fish which have been taken from many of the loughs and stretches of rivers within the area. The second feature is water clarity. Some waters such as Lough Ennell are so clear that on a bright calm day it is no difficult feat to view underwater clusters of rocks, resembling over-baked loaves, stretching out for many yards into the lough. Even on such a lough as Corrib, whose waters do not have such a high alkaline content as those of Ennell, one can view underwater growth perhaps twelve feet below the surface, with the utmost facility. As previously mentioned, there are large areas of bogland in the Central Plain, but except during flood conditions when turbid waters run from the bogs, the waters are generally so clear that a wary approach is necessary on the part of the angler.

Water pollution or interference are not unknown in Ireland, but the country is not heavily industrialised, and its waters have generally remained pure and undisturbed, save through natural processes. Occasionally the level of certain loughs has been lowered, and rivers dredged for purposes of drainage, but these acts have been on a rather limited scale, and thus, in the main, the coarse fish have not only been able to exist, but also to breed, unmolested by humanity, except in certain specific waters which are being developed for the benefit of the trout angler.

The small population of Ireland, and the general availability of game fishing, are other factors which have doubtless retarded the development of Irish coarse fishing. The population of the whole of Ireland is under 4,500,000, and a large proportion of the country's inhabitants live in the cities and towns which are mainly situated in the coastal regions. Trout fishing is not only widespread, but can be obtained at a very reasonable cost, if indeed a payment has to be made, and is of such a standard that coarse fishing has generally been neglected and, indeed, is only practised by a minority group of Ireland's freshwater anglers. However, because of the increased publicity given to this branch of angling, and because of a general interest which has materialised from observing the activities of visiting anglers, coarse fishing is being practised more freely now by the home population than at any time in the country's history.

Coarse fish have long been known to frequent Irish waters, but roach and dace have only appeared there within the last century. These latter fish and also carp and tench were, no doubt, introduced for purposes of consumption, ornamentation, or for use as bait to lure other fish. Of the coarse fish found in Ireland, pride of place, from the point of view of numbers, is held by the perch, although the trout is actually the most widely distributed of all the freshwater fishes. Until some seven or eight years after the Second World War, the pike was the most sought after coarse fish, but in the last decade I feel it has lost its place to the bream. This fish is keenly angled for by many visiting anglers, and again several erstwhile first-class pike waters are being developed in the interests of trout fishing. The pike, however, still remains first choice among Irish coarse fishermen.

Concerning the distribution of coarse fish, whereas they can be found in certain coastal regions, most of the country's coarse fishing is performed in inland areas which comprise a large portion of Ireland. I should say that about one-half of the northern section of Eire, and about one-sixth of the southern part of the whole country are capable of providing coarse fishing. Northern Ireland has many waters, of which the best known are probably Upper and Lower Lough Erne, and Lough Neagh.

The northern counties of the Republic are extremely rich in coarse fish waters. The upper-central and mid-western districts are also of importance to the coarse fisherman, but with the exception of one important area in County Clare, the bulk of Ireland's still-water coarse fishing is found in the aforementioned areas. There are numerous loughs in the south, south-east, and also south-west, but only a very few are of interest to the coarse fisherman. All the large loughs contain coarse fish, but there are waters within the coarse angling districts, from which certain of the more popular species of fish are either absent, or only exist in small numbers.

One sometimes encounters loughs of minor acreage where such fish as rudd and perch are numerous, although their average size is small, but certain small loughs can provide excellent fishing.

I recall being led by the young son of a friend of mine, to a tiny lough in County Cavan some years ago. The lough was barely two acres in size and for the most part its banks were lined with bulrushes, and as a result of frequent showers were extremely muddy. It was a typically small bog lough with dark, still waters, and my young, experienced guide shepherded me through the tall meadow grass to a spot where there was a gap between the rushes. I commenced fishing and almost every cast produced a rudd, and my total catch, which included some quite large fish, was considerable. This is only one of many pleasant days I have spent fishing at such waters and they are well worth exploring. One, however, does not come across ponds very often in Ireland. Nature has dotted the central plain with many loughs, which by Irish standards are deemed to be on the small side, but they are invariably larger than the average English meadow pond.

Certain districts seem to produce a lough at every bend in the road; other districts have not been so well served by nature. They vary in character and may have partially or wholly boggy, stony or reed-lined shores, or perhaps shores where meadowland reaches right down to the water's edge.

Whereas the greatest individual concentration of large freshwater loughs is found on the Atlantic side of Ireland, in the shapes of Loughs Corrib, Mask, Carra and Conn, an extremely impressive stretch of water known as Lough Ree is found right in the heart of the country, and it is the most striking feature of the Great Plain, being approximately fifteen miles in length. This lough, together with Loughs Derg, Allen and other smaller loughs, form part of the Shannon system, its main tributaries being the Suck, the Boyle, the Inny and the Brosna.

Much as the Central Plain and its environs dominate the coarse fishing scene, there are many loughs and rivers elsewhere containing coarse fish. Flowing peacefully through the hinterland of the south-eastern part of the country are the Rivers Nore and Barrow, and there is the River Blackwater which passes through certain of the southern counties. All the aforementioned waterways will be discussed more fully later, but from the general description already given it can be seen that coarse fishing is available on a wide scale.

The climate is usually kind to the angler, and whereas I would not hide the fact that Ireland does experience periods of drought or continuous rain, these features are reasonably common to the whole of the British Isles, and are accepted by anglers as part of their heritage. One must be prepared to experience changeable weather during any reasonable period of time throughout the seasons, although the statistically minded person may be interested to learn that the warmest weather occurs during July and August when the temperature averages approximately 60 degrees Fahrenheit, and it reaches its lowest average in February when it falls to about 40 degrees Fahrenheit. The eastern side of the country has less rain than the west, and the southern counties tend to enjoy more sunshine than those in the north. I cannot, however, recommend any period in the year when the weather is likely to be "reasonably settled", for as previously stated, the weather can change from day to day, or even in a matter of an hour or less; and I would emphasise this point owing to the fact that a certain amount of coarse fishing is performed from boats in Ireland, and sudden winds can take boat anglers unawares, and at the least, cause moments of unpleasantness. Such anglers should respect not only the open stretches of the bigger loughs, but also the straight sections of the wider parts of rivers, where a combination of strong wind and current can cause anxiety. One should not venture out on any of Ireland's principal loughs without first seeking local advice, unless the services of a ghillie have been obtained, and warm clothing should always be available.

Anglers who frequently fish in Ireland learn to understand the peculiarities of the climate and they adapt themselves accordingly. The brilliant sunshine, the strong winds, the alternating periods of brightness and showers, the high clouds racing in from the Atlantic. the morning mists, the coolness of the lough and the softness of the air are all familiar features of Ireland's weather. The fly, the spinner, the leger and the float are changed as regularly as the weather changes, and such acts are performed by the regular angler without real concern or comment, but rather with a quiet acceptance and appreciation of the Irish angling way of life.

Some years ago I visited Ireland during late April and early May for the joint purposes of enjoying some trout fishing and of observing the habits of the coarse fish at this time of the year. The last days of April were so cold that it was necessary to don just about every piece of clothing I had brought with me. The first week in May, however, brought days of clear, blue skies, and high temperatures. Weather, in fact, which is often described by the Englishman as "glorious", and the Irishman as "desperate". During that week, bream drifted aimlessly along the stretches of canals, and pike lay on the water surface like logs. Bream in the local rivers hung like immobile saucers around the weed beds, and only the rudd seemed to appreciate the warmth and brilliance of the days. I recall returning to this district during the following September and the two rivers there were in spate! Within three days, however, they were fishable once more, and the late season trout fishing and general coarse fishing were both of a high standard. Such is Ireland of the unpredictable, fascinating and lively climate.

Chapter Two

THE COARSE FISH OF IRELAND

Common Bream

THE BREAM is undoubtedly the most popular of the coarse fish found in Ireland. It grows to an excellent size and is renowned for its fighting qualities, and is found in nearly all of the areas which coarse fish inhabit. There is only one species of bream in Ireland, and I mention this point as small bream are often caught that are whitish in appearance, and they are sometimes mistakenly considered to be silver bream. Such bream lose their silver colouring by the time they have reached a fair weight, and they then assume the more familiar bronze appearance.

The study of the Irish bream is a fascinating occupation, especially during the breeding season, when they congregate in large shoals to reproduce their kind, and later travel to the faster water, if it exists, to scour themselves, leaving the water at intervals to return with a pulse-tingling splash or else glide along just below the surface, exposing their dorsal fins as they travel on their way in such determined fashion. It is at this period of the year that the otherwise sober and retiring bream may assume the role of predator. It has been known to fall easy prey to the spoon and spinner, which are normally reserved for the capture of the official predators. This is an extreme aspect of bream fishing in Ireland, but it proves that smaller fish have more to contend with than just the cannibalistic activities of larger pike, perch and trout.

There is little difference between the methods used for fishing for bream in Ireland and England. Such fish are rarely sluggish and are often located in fast water, so one must not regard them as being "still water" fish.

The more enthusiastic of the angling fraternity concentrate on early morning, late evening and night fishing. This is, fortunately, not an essential rule, however, and far too many catches have been made during the daylight hours for one to suggest otherwise. A sharp fall in temperature at dusk can be responsible for the bream going off feed, and they may not be responsive again until the sun is quite high on the following day. Even after a warm evening, the arrival of a fresh breeze during the ensuing day may well cause bream to continue to feed, although the day in question is bright. The still, hot, cloudless day is the one the bream angler finds most frustrating, but he may achieve success as a result of searching the deeper waters and glides of rivers, or some silt-covered bed lying below the deep waters of a lough, or indeed, certain weed-strewn shallows.

The average size of bream differs from one area to another in Ireland, as one might expect, but this can be the case on individual waterways. I know of a certain river where bream average about $2\frac{1}{2}$ lb. in weight along one stretch, yet some miles down its course the average weight rises to 4 lb. Farther downstream again, the weight is about 3 lb. Larger fish are caught from time to time, but these average weights have remained quite constant through the years. I would also mention that small bream are rarely caught although they are obviously there and this fact particularly applies to the country's rivers.

Bream are sometimes caught quite unexpectedly, and I recall that this was the case once, when boat fishing for perch. The perch shoal had moved from where it had been located and upon searching the immediate area, the bait of redworm was readily accepted by bream. Half a dozen were hooked and they were really excellent fish. I discovered that the stony river bed, where the perch were found, shelved off to form a muddy bottom with a certain amount of weed growth, and there the bream had elected to stop, much to the delight of those present.

Each year specimen bream are caught and some are submitted to the Irish Specimen Fish Committee for their consideration. In 1961, for example, six such fish were included in the

Committee's published list, and they weighed between 7 lb. 1 oz. and 8 lb. 9¼ oz. They were all caught during the month of July, and five of them were taken from the River Suck. This does not give a fair indication of Irish bream fishing, either from the point of view of location or time. There are many waters capable of producing specimen bream, and the peak of the bream fishing season does not particularly fall around July. The standard of bream fishing on the River Suck, however, has never been disputed, and it may be convenient to mention here that the first organised body of coarse fishing anglers to visit Ireland, went to Ballinasloe on this river. The record Irish bream is a splendid specimen of 11 lb. 12 oz., and there is no doubt in the minds of those people who are freely connected with Irish coarse fishing that this weight is quite capable of being emulated.

Bream fishing is undoubtedly the yard-stick by which coarse fishing in this country is measured. This form of angling above all others combines quality with quantity, and it is enormously popular with visiting anglers. The large number of persons who arrive each year, mainly with the object of seeking such fish, still surprises many of the local inhabitants at angling centres, yet such people come with the knowledge that their predecessors, as a whole, have been reasonably successful, and it is their intention to enjoy a similar standard of angling. Whatever one may say about the expression "coarse fishing", I am extremely grateful that the Irish bream has never become an Irish delicacy, and because of this, the majority of such fish swim on, as year follows year, ready to provide the angler with first-class sport and worthwhile memories.

The Perch

Although it is untrue to say that every second fish caught in Ireland is most likely to be a perch, the fact of the matter is that most of the loughs and rivers in the coarse fishing districts of the country contain perch, and the only regrettable thing about it is that their average size tends to be on the small side.

There are certain waters where many good perch are to be found, however, and as mentioned in the previous chapter, if the visiting angler is near to such a place, he should certainly allot part of his time to the act of perch fishing, as there is no more satisfying sight in angling than that of a large perch lying safely in the landing net.

The Irish perch is forever like its English cousin. It readily accepts worm and maggot, and a hesitant strike invariably means that the disgorger must be put to use. It enjoys the proximity of stones and gravel, and in their absence will most certainly be found near to the river bank among the reeds and lily pads. They rarely allow one to become impatient, and in some rivers I have formed the opinion that there is at least one perch allocated to every half-foot of bank! There are times when they persistently attack lobworms and maggots intended for other fish, and although one feels indignant at the time, one ultimately realises that they do much to maintain one's interest, and they are sometimes responsible for preventing what would otherwise be a blank day.

No doubt the presence of such a large number of small perch is the result of their being able to breed so prolifically in the vast stretches of water there, although the size of their ancestors was probably never particularly large either. Nevertheless, fine perch are to be found, and although one may come across a specimen fish purely by good fortune, as for example when spinning for pike and legering for bream, there are several waters where large perch are regularly caught by design.

Two rivers which are well known for producing good perch are the River Suck and the River Inny. Loughs Arrow, Key, Cloonacleigha and Gowna are outstanding waters in this respect and some of the country's main loughs, namely Conn and Mask, have provided excellent perch fishing, but it must be remembered that in more recent years, numerous perch have been removed in an endeavour to improve the trout fishing there.

A fair percentage of the total number of big perch which have come to net have been taken by anglers primarily fishing for pike and trout; and these acts of chance, coupled with the facts that the general average size of the Irish perch is small, that the larger fish are caught, on the whole, in certain well-defined areas, and that the coarse fisherman is often quite content to angle for other species, are probably the reasons why perch fishing is considered to be subordinate to other angling practices. Whatever the general feeling may be, the Irish perch can provide pleasant, interesting fishing, and the small perch can be caught with such ease, and by so many methods, that in normal conditions the angler should rarely be frustrated.

Worm or maggot fished near to river bank or lough shore have produced the majority of perch caught in Ireland, but I have caught fine perch from the deeper waters of loughs, using leger tackle, and also from the faster waters of rivers, running over stone or gravel, with the same tackle. I also have vivid memories of perch fishing from the rocky bays and shores of several Irish loughs, particularly during autumn when perch, in incredible numbers, congregate there, before moving off to the depths.

The larger perch, save during their periodic raids on fry, do not show themselves quite as readily, or are indeed, quite as nomadic as large rudd, bream or pike, and this is possibly another reason why specimen perch fishing is still something of an unknown quantity in Ireland; but I would stress the point that if one is informed about the presence of such fish in a lough or river near to where one is staying, no harm will come from investigating the water concerned, and one's act could add an interesting chapter to the story of the country's perch fishing.

The Pike

It is perhaps surprising that in over forty years no one has ever emulated John Garvin's feat of legitimately capturing a 53 lb. pike in Ireland. From time to time one hears stories of pike over that weight being seen, or caught, but the record remains intact, as the other fearsome monsters are either cut up for pig food, or indeed for human consumption, or else vanish in some mysterious way before their weight and capture can be authenticated. There will always be stories related about the existence of such large fish, and I, for one, shall never tire of listening to them, but it is a fact that since 1920 the record has not been broken, and it is also a fact that visiting anglers have been keenly joining in the search for a new record fish, in ever increasing numbers for at least a decade, and their efforts have been fruitless, although an abundance of fish have been caught. However, as previously mentioned, each lough and river has its own peculiarities, and each day its own weather, and they merit the utmost consideration before deciding how to fish.

It is a strong tradition that in Ireland one trolls for pike. Dead bait, artificial bait and boat are quite inseparable, and if the river is in spate, or the weather is "contrary", neither boat nor rod are put into motion. The season commences when the weather becomes settled, which may or may not be during the English close season, and it generally terminates by October. During this period, limitless numbers of pike are caught, and a large percentage of them are taken from the proximity of weed beds which stretch along many of the lough shores and river banks of Ireland. There is a tendency for the line to be of a high breaking strain and the rod to be of solid proportions, and I fancy that few pike are returned to the water after being caught. The local anglers are methodical, confident, wary and shrewd. The pike to them is either a ruthless enemy, or else a rather commonplace sort of vermin, ever available for removal from the waters wherein it swims, and is looked upon far more for its food value or as an enemy of trout than as a provider of sport.

The visiting angler may or may not consider this fish from the point of view of sport only. Pike fishing has reached its climax in Ireland. Tons of pike have been removed from the main trout waters, although I would stress the point that there are many waters that have not been professionally netted and this includes virtually all the recognised coarse fish loughs and rivers. Perhaps one day a new and exciting fish will be entered into the record books. As no 50-pounders have been netted during the past ten years, it could well be that the ghost of the Lough Conn monster will still triumphantly swim in the waters of that inland sea for some time yet!

The Rudd

If I had received a small gratuity for every rudd I had caught in Ireland I would be an extremely solvent piscator, but I never tire of rudd fishing and I shall always be grateful for their presence in Ireland because they, like their colleagues the perch, have often provided an excellent day's sport when other species of fish have been in fastidious mood. I am not inferring that rudd should be angled for only when other fish are not feeding, but that of the recognised species of coarse fish in Ireland, the rudd is the one which is most often likely to accommodate and delight the angler.

This is because apart from being found in most waters containing coarse fish, it will, in addition, accept a number of baits at various depths, and is usually not especially concerned about survival. I would also add that as it often feeds and plays on the surface of lough and river, it is easily located, and it will feed in many conditions of weather and water, and is willing to swim in waters where there is a reasonable current. Its whereabouts are not, therefore, particularly restricted.

The above remarks may suggest that the capture of rudd is a mere formality, so I therefore make the following additional comments. The larger rudd, like adult perch and bream, gains wisdom with age. It is a magnificent fish and has little desire to display its fine appearance from the inside of a glass case. Although it may attach itself to a shoal of its younger brethren and act as sentinel, its sagacity renders it difficult to catch, and I know of few fish whose presence is so apparent but whose desire to live is so great. The other rudd, too, often frustrate the

angler, for by virtue of their nomadic outlook on life, they sometimes depart from their lair without special reason and leave
the angler casting his bait into fishless waters.

My own experience prompts me to say that such fish often
tend to form select bands and enjoy an adult existence together,
although one must expect to fish shoals of varying sizes from
time to time, and when one casts ones bait among them, it is
invariably the younger brethren who get to it first! Having experimented with baits over a reasonable number of years, I have
come to the conclusion that extra large portions of most baits
are near the complete answer to the capture of the biggest fish.
They certainly frustrate the fry, but they do not over-concern
the others, at least as far as a moving bait is concerned. If
one must suggest a reason, I suppose the answer is that the idea
of a full-blooded lobworm or golf-ball sized piece of paste passing through their ranks, does nothing more than interest them,
and that redworm, a couple of maggots or a "sensible" piece of
bread crust are far too acceptable to other fish. The specimen
hunter who lays on for them, or who is fortunate enough to find
them in a confined space, ironically enough, is capable of suc-
ceeding with smaller baits, but in other waters and situations,
something a little more "suspicious" and less orthodox is the
rule. The same idea applies to the use of groundbait. If the shoal
is unaffected by one's activities, groundbait is not only a superfluous item but may have harmful effects. On the other hand,
if the shoal is in rather a lethargic mood, or tending to roam,
a small amount of groundbait designed to attract and adminis-
tered at conservative intervals is desirable.

Although rudd shoals in Ireland vary in size, it is interesting
to note that time after time one comes across shoals where the
weight of the individual fish is uniform, in the main, and it
can be from $\frac{1}{4}$ lb. to $1\frac{1}{2}$ lb. Fish over the latter weight are more
difficult to locate, but happy is the angler who finds a number
of two-pounders in taking mood. There are certainly a reasonable number of fine rudd of that weight and over in this country, but it must be remembered that rudd-bream hybrids exist

Netting a fish on the River Shannon by Lough Forbes, County Longford

and that any large fish caught should be closely examined to ascertain whether or not it is a true rudd. If the upper lip protrudes or the anal fin is bream-like in appearance, it is most assuredly a hybrid.

Just as the sight of a 2 lb. rudd is one of the most satisfying in angling (especially if the fish is in the landing net!), so is the sight of a large shoal of rudd one of the most fascinating, and the angler who visits Ireland should sooner or later come across one of them. Obviously the day must be bright and the water reasonably calm and clear, but once having seen such a congregation of fish, he will appreciate the number of rudd that can be found in one shoal. One tends to associate really large shoals with the spawning season, but I have seen rudd assembled in countless numbers in September and October. When fishing for rudd in peat waters or swims whose waters are agitated by wind, the number of fish present cannot be assessed with any degree of accuracy, but it is possible to catch rudd in one given stretch of lake or river for hours on end, and the shoal in question seems boundless and its activities endless.

The rudd is occasionally caught on leger tackle and sometimes during the hours of darkness. It can be quite easily caught on fly, and with a dapped bluebottle, but light float tackle takes priority, to my mind, especially when fishing a gently flowing swim fringed with lily pads, and with the temperature pleasantly high, and a brightness in the air.

Those who regularly visit Ireland experience many such occasions, and they are an essential part of Irish coarse fishing. They are also some of the most enjoyable encountered, and apart from the fact that near surface fishing or mid-water fishing is something of a novelty to many English anglers, the size and number of this species of fish, which are so readily available, render the act of rudd fishing a necessary part of one's fishing activities in the country.

C

Other Fish

The remaining coarse fish found in Ireland and of interest
to the angler are carp, roach, dace, pope and gudgeon. Eels,
thwaite shad and flounders however, are also found in fresh
water, and chub, so I was once told, have been caught in one
area, but this allegation has, to my knowledge, never been
substantiated.

Because of its quiet disposition, its act of seasonal hibernation
and its reluctance to show itself to all and sundry, the Irish
tench has only recently received the publicity given to pike,
perch, bream and rudd. This fish, however, has been located
over a wide section of the Shannon system and in several loughs,
and it is openly acknowledged that some excellent specimens
are to be found in Ireland. Certain suitable loughs and other
waterways have been stocked with tench, and carp, too, have
been introduced to new waters, and these acts are definite indi-
cations that there is a sincere desire upon the part of those concerned with Irish coarse fishing, to improve and expand the
coarse fishing potential of the country. In future time it may be
true to say that the majority of coarse fish waters will have their
head of tench. They have been caught at such centres as Meelick, Banagher, Lanesborough and Kilglass on the River Shannon system. Certain lakes at Carrigallen, Arva, Lough Gowna,
Ballybay, Multyfarnham and Carrickmacross contain tench
as do the Dysart Lakes and ponds outside Thurles. Bearing in
mind that the aforementioned locations are situated as far
north as County Monaghan and as far south as County
Tipperary, a glance at the map will show that tench are to be
found over a large area of the country.

Irish tench fishing still has rather shallow roots, as it were,
and it is to be hoped that the capture of any good fish of this
species, will be properly recorded so as to assist the authorities
in their investigations concerning this fish.

Dace and roach were accidentally introduced into the famous
River Blackwater during the nineteenth century. The dace

has been the more prolific breeder, and in some districts local anglers have told me that their presence has seriously jeopardised trout fishing. I have seen several shoals containing vast numbers of these fish, and huge catches have been made by visiting anglers from time to time. In addition to "enjoying" the comforts and the scenic beauty of this game river, dace also grow to a good average size and fight well on light tackle. They will accept a fly quite freely, as well as the baits usually associated with dace fishing, and long trotting for these sporting fish is an enjoyable pastime.

The roach there are not as plentiful, nor make their presence known as freely as do the dace, but certain districts provide excellent roach fishing, and some very good fish have been caught. Of the towns and villages along the banks of the River Blackwater, Fermoy, in particular, has been developed as a coarse fishing angling centre, and in addition to roach and dace, perch and pike are found there. Cappoquin, at the tidal head of the River, is another popular centre, and dace, in particular, are extremely numerous. Flounders, eels, trout, and in season, sea trout, are also caught there, and when legering with worms, one never really knows which species of fish is going to accept one's bait.

Eels are plentiful in Ireland, and they readily find their way into the country's rivers and loughs. The rivers Shannon and Barrow, as much as any other waterway, have provided anglers with many anxious moments after hooking a large eel on light tackle, and the visiting angler must be prepared, sooner or later, to find this fish firmly secured to his hook. Many large eels are caught and there always seems to be a local resident about, who considers them to be a delicacy and who will readily accept them for consumption.

From this and the previous chapter, one will conclude that the act of coarse fishing in Ireland can produce fish of good individual weight and fish in quantity. Visitors who have spent most of their angling life in search of roach and dace will be able to enjoy the delights of rudd and bream fishing, and may well experience tench and pike fishing for the first time. It should also be remembered that in Ireland trout are often to be found in those sections of rivers and certain loughs known principally for their head of coarse fish, and thus, any obvious indication of their presence should be investigated, provided, of course, one is lawfully entitled to fish for them. A change is as good as a rest, even in the world of coarse fishing, and a goodly trout is a worthwhile acquisition!

Chapter Three

A VARIETY OF VENUES

I WOULD NOW like to refer to the various coarse fishing districts
and some of their angling centres. The growth of the latter
has been pronounced in the past years, and there is today an
excellent choice of centres available for those anglers who wish
to visit this land of quiet charm and refreshing peacefulness,
where to relax is an order, and to enjoy oneself is a command.

I would divide Ireland into six areas, and refer to them as
the northern counties of Eire, Northern Ireland, the Shannon
basin, the western lakes, the Westmeath Lake District and
lastly the rivers Blackwater and Barrow. The most complex is
the Northern area where a great number of lakes and an incredible waterway known as the Erne River system are to be
found. The Shannon system is, on the other hand, the most impressive waterway in Great Britain and Ireland, and it would
take many lifetimes to appreciate it fully. The western lakes,
which principally consist of loughs Corrib, Mask and Conn, are
magnificent inland seas, ever powerful and mysterious and a
challenge to the hardy angler. The Westmeath Lakes have their
own character, and the attention they have from the mayfly,
tench and pike specialists, as well as the general angler, grows
annually. Lastly, there is that phenomenon, the River Blackwater with its private stock of roach and dace, which has en-
ticed many anglers to its water's edge, and the River Barrow
which is the only other main waterway of interest to coarse
fisherman in this area of Ireland.

Although some will, no doubt, disagree with the way in which
I have elected to divide the country, my journeys across Ireland
during past years have caused me to consider the position thus.

It is impossible here to refer to all of the established angling centres, but mention of a few from each district will give the intending visitor an idea of the various facilities available, and a general impression of each district.

In the northern counties, the towns of Ballybay, Lough Gowna, Ballinamore, and Belturbet easily come to mind. Each has a number of lakes and a river nearby, and the landscape is one of narrow lanes, minor hills, copses and well-defined meadowland. The emphasis here is on still water fishing, perhaps in quiet bays and with one's float lying among the lily pads, or near to the reeds, and cast from even banks. The bream and rudd thrive in prodigious numbers and one may have a lake or two to oneself during the whole of one's stay. The slow-moving rivers render fishing effortless, and one soon feels "at home", either in the meadows, or while walking alongside the hedgerows. The northern angling centres are so numerous that one could spend a month travelling to a new one each day, and still not visit them all. If one excludes the upper section of the River Shannon, to which reference will shortly be made, there remains an area which may be divided into three sections, namely the Sligo, Upper Erne, and north-east lakeland districts. Of these, the first named is the least complex, in that there are but four centres of note. Firstly, there is Ballymote, situated near the Owenmore River and several loughs, including Templehouse and Cloonacleigha, which provide excellent pike and perch fishing. Then there is the county town of Sligo with the adjoining Lough Gill, which holds a good stock of both coarse and game fish, and lastly there are Kiltyclogher and Manorhamilton, which are convenient centres for fishing upper and lower Lough Macnean and the river which joins them. These are really excellent coarse fishing waters, and amongst the finest which are to be found in Ireland.

The central northern section contains several well-known centres which are situated on the Erne system, or on either side thereof. This system is an extremely complicated mass of water, and the "confusion", if I may use this word, commences right at its source, where, on its eastern side, is situated the village of Gowna, which used to be called Scrabby, but has now assumed the name of the lough which lies below it. The River Erne flows rather unpretentiously from the lough for some miles, passing Arva, near to which are several excellent loughs, until it enters the watery maze known as Lough Oughter and to the east and west are, respectively, Cavan Town and Killeshandra. Carrigallen, some miles to the south-west of Killesandra, is a pleasant village with four loughs nearby, and the quality of the fishing they have produced, has brought much praise from visiting anglers. There are tench in two of the local waters and as one of them produced a former record fish of precisely 7 lb., it may be seen that Carrigallen is one of the leading tench districts in Ireland. Mohill, to the south-west, is another fine centre.

Between Lough Oughter and Upper Lough Erne are Milltown, and one of Ireland's pioneering angling centres, Belturbet, where many heavy catches of bream have been made on the Erne. Mention must be made of Ballyconnell, lying on the Woodford River to the east of Belturbet, and another popular centre, as previously mentioned, Ballinamore which is near to Lough Garadice. This is one of the largest loughs in the area and was chosen as a venue for one of the All-Ireland angling competitions. Just north of Belturbet is the Border dividing the Republic of Ireland from the six counties of Northern Ireland. Here one finds the beginning of Upper Lough Erne with the towns of Newtown Butler, Lisnaskea and Maguires Bridge nearby. Lower Lough Erne is found some ten miles farther along the course of this waterway. The lough is situated between the towns of Enniskillen and Belleek, with Pettigo on its northern shore, and is almost twenty miles in length. These two formidable stretches of water contain bream, perch, rudd, pike and trout of the highest quality, and like many other waters in Ireland, much as their value is known, their story is only really beginning to be told.

There are several rivers and many loughs in Northern Ireland

containing coarse fish and one interesting point is that roach
exist. The Fairy Water, as it is generally known, has gained a
fair reputation in more recent years for the quality of its roach
fishing.

Lough Neagh holds innumerable coarse fish, but because of
its immense size, anglers may well prefer to fish its tributary
streams. The River Blackwater, for example, provides excellent
pike, bream and perch fishing, and convenient centres are
Dungannon and Benburb. Near the former town is Black Lough
which holds large pike.

The local loughs of Lisburn in County Down also provide
good pike fishing, and it is very true to say that in Northern
Ireland the spinning enthusiast in particular does not have to
look very hard to find suitable waters.

Traversing the Border again, we come to the last of the northern sections which comprises those centres in east Cavan and
Monaghan.

Bailieborough is perhaps the oldest centre, with its own Town
Lough, and nearby Castle Lake but nowadays the towns of
Ballybay, Ballyjamesduff, Carrickmacross, Clones, Kingscourt,
Cootehill, the county town of Monaghan, and Shercock and
Castleblaney, as aforementioned, are all well known to visiting
anglers. There is also the small town of Virginia, almost on the
shore of Lough Ramor, and this lough, apart from being extremely attractive, and some five miles in length, is well stocked
with coarse fish and trout, and I recall that excellent catches of
perch have been made in the vicinity of the outflowing River
Blackwater.

Several loughs in this north-eastern section of the Republic
have gained a fair reputation as a result of the excellent catches
of fish which have been made by anglers, but it would perhaps
be unfair to make special reference to them, owing to the fact
that such results could so easily have occurred elsewhere. I say
this quite sincerely, for I have fished many loughs in this area,
and whereas results have not always been satisfactory, which
was due to my own shortcomings as an angler as much as any

other factor, the general impression I have formed of these waters is that the quality of their fishing is of a very high standard indeed. The main point is that one fishes with a high degree of confidence, owing to the fact that the loughs are, as often as not, of reasonably small acreage, which assists in the act of fish location. I refer to bream and rudd in particular, and these fish have reached a high average size in the fertile waters under discussion. The district is not without waters of the more imposing type. Loughs Muckno, Sillan, the lonely and marshy Egish, and perhaps Tacker and Ross, fall into this category, but I prefer to think of the area as one of sheltered, informal, intimate lakes, hidden by wood or hillock, which are as often as not quite willing to reveal their fish when discovered by the angler.

The bream in Lough Major, close to Ballybay, can satisfy any angler's appetite. Those who have fished the loughs surrounding Carrickmacross have not infrequently spent the day filling their keep nets. The 10 lb. 11 oz. bream which quite openly accepted an artificial lure cast into the waters of Lough na Glack, near to this town, has become a legend in a few short years. If one enjoys spinning for perch and also eating large blackberries, then one should take the north road from Kingscourt on a September day and make a circular tour of Lough Greaghlone. If one really wants to feel alone, and like Lamartine, "Listen to the lapping of the waters", then one should follow the map, very carefully, from Shercock and stop beside Lough Namacree. Truly, this area has much to offer the angler.

As a complete contrast I would now turn to the Shannon River system. The River Shannon is the longest river in Britain and Ireland and one soon learns to consider it as an endless waterway, for ever disappearing into the horizon. It sometimes transforms itself into lakeland, sometimes into a maze of channels and islands, and from time to time it greets the presence of waters from some in-flowing river. Except at certain notable places, its flow is even paced during normal conditions, from its source in the Leitrim hills to its southernmost regions.

To the boatman, angler and wildfowler alike, it is a world unto itself, with its low banks, heavy reed beds and dark waters, and the loughs along its course become dangerous when agitated by storm.

Certain stretches of the River Shannon are very sparsely populated and at other places one may only see the occasional farmhouse or cottage. Along its course, however, there are a considerable number of towns and villages, and many of them now answer the call of the angler. In the immediate post-war years, only perhaps Carrick and Athlone were reasonably well-known to the coarse fisherman. Banagher and Clondara subsequently gained in popularity, and nowadays there are at least a dozen centres freely visited by anglers.

Drumshanbo is the most northerly of the centres. It is situated at the lower end of temperamental Lough Allen and about two miles from the river, and is thus convenient for fishing both waters. A few miles south of Drumshanbo is the small town of Leitrim, and farther south again one comes across Carrick with its narrow main street and well-known quayside and bridge. The waters of the River Shannon hereabouts are among the best known in Ireland. Enormous catches of bream have been made there, and many large pike have been taken.

Here it is convenient to refer to the River Boyle, which is found to the west of Carrick. It connects Lough Gara with Lough Key and between these two waters is the town of Boyle itself. From Lough Key the river proceeds in a south-easterly direction through Oakport Lough and Lough Drumharlow where it meets the River Shannon. This is an excellent coarse fishing area, and let it not be forgotten that Lough Arrow is but four miles from Boyle, and although it is best known for its big trout, coarse fish thrive in its waters.

Proceeding down the River Shannon from Carrick, one shortly finds Jamestown and Drumsna, which are situated on a rather pronounced bend of the river. Many years ago a canal was constructed here, joining the respective lower sections of the bend for the benefit of rivercraft, and it contains a fair head

of coarse fish. Rooskey is the next centre of note, and many
bream are to be found in the river there. North of this village
are Loughs Bofin and Boderg, which are exposed waters and
they quickly gain in fury when the north wind blows. There is a
waterway leading into Lough Boderg from the west, whose
source is Kilglass Lake. It is joined to Lower Grange Lough by
a disused canal, which I have never been able to find at its
northern end, owing to an amazing profusion of reeds. Upper
Grange Lough is in close attendance, and all these waters provide excellent coarse fishing. I would add that there are fine
tench hereabouts, and also trout. Strokestown is a convenient
centre for fishing this "off-shoot" of the Shannon River system,
and there are several other very good lakes in the vicinity.

Below Rooskey is Lough Forbes with the in-flowing River
Rinn, and then one eventually encounters Tarmonbarry,
which is on the River Shannon itself, and Clondara, close to the
eastern side of the river. As previously stated, Clondara is one
of the original coarse fishing centres and its popularity is in no
small way due to the fact that here the River Camlin joins the
River Shannon. This is one of Ireland's best minor rivers and it
has produced very good bream and pike.

Several miles south of Clondara is Lanesborough, which is
conveniently situated at the head of Lough Ree, on the eastern
bank of the River Shannon. Lough Ree is one of Ireland's largest stretches of water, and one cannot say more than that it
contains unlimited numbers of coarse fish, and is ideal for the
type of angler who is prepared to "brave the storm" and who is
desirous of searching unknown depths. The town of Athlone is
an ideal centre for fishing the lower section of the lough. It has
long been used to catering for the needs of anglers, and the sections of the River Shannon above and below the town merit
special mention, for there are fine specimens of bream, pike and
rudd in these waters.

Here, reference must be made to the River Inny which enters
Lough Ree on its eastern side. Several loughs are found along
the course of this river, which wanders pleasantly through the

counties of Westmeath and Longford. These loughs will be
discussed later and as for the River Inny itself, the angler soon
finds that he is concerned with a river of constantly changing
character. Sometimes it is canal-like in appearance, with short
reeds and lily pads suggesting the presence of rudd, or else it
resembles a Broadland dyke, lonely and half-hidden by marsh
grass. Along other sections its flow increases, and its waters pass
over stone beds and suggest the presence of trout. Ballymahon,
Ballynagarrigy, Finea and Castlepollard are convenient centres for fishing this most interesting of Irish rivers. It must be
noted however that at the present time, drainage operations are
affecting angling.

Reverting to the River Shannon, the next centre is some miles
south of Athlone, although mention must be made of the small
village of Shannonbridge, just below which the River Suck joins
the main waterway. Shannonbridge may be reached from Ballinasloe, Ferbane, or from Banagher. This latter town, with its
rising main street, and generous bridge across the mighty river,
has long been devoted to accommodating the angling visitor.
A couple of miles to the north of Banagher is Shannon Harbour
where the River Brosna enters the River Shannon and through
which passes the Grand Canal on its journey from Dublin to
Ballinasloe. Hereabouts, there is much good fishing to be
enjoyed.

Below Banagher is the hamlet of Meelick where the River
Shannon transforms itself into a maze of waterways, which are
worthy of investigation by the angler. About six miles south of
Meelick the river flows into Lough Derg, which is renowned
for its trout fishing. Its fine pike, and great shoals of rudd and
bream, however, also attract the coarse fisherman, and accommodation is available at Portumna, Mountshannon, Dromi-
neer, and at Killaloe which is situated on the river, just below
the point where it leaves Lough Derg. Between Killaloe and
Limerick Town there is good coarse fishing, and this is the last
part of the system which concerns the coarse angler, for just
above Limerick the water is tidal.

Before concluding this brief description of the Shannon River system, I must refer to the River Suck which is the Shannon's longest tributary. It owes its popularity to two main factors. The first, as one may imagine, is the high standard of its coarse fishing, and the second is, that the town of Ballinasloe, situate on the lower reaches of the river, has been visited by anglers for a considerable number of years. At this point on the Suck, and for the remaining ten or so miles of its course, some of its best fishing is found, and although there are coarse fish in the river north of Ballinasloe, this town except Ballygar is really the only recognised angling centre found along its banks. The river has several stretches which consist of glides and broken water, and which can provide good trout fishing. The whole of the fishing, incidentally, is controlled by the Inland Fisheries Trust, and thus, both trout and coarse anglers are required to provide themselves with a permit.

The western loughs of Ireland are well known to game and coarse fishermen alike. Including the numerous lakes around Corofin in County Clare, the various stretches of water in which coarse fish are to be found, are spread over a distance of about ninety miles, and it is to be imagined that an angler who is accustomed to fishing quiet streams and placid lakes, would be quite intrigued with the prospect of trying his luck on Lough Corrib, which alone is twenty-seven miles long. The fishing here, and on the other great lakes is, of course, boundless, and local advice can be invaluable in connection with the location of bream and rudd. Certain bays and stretches of shore are quite shallow in normal conditions, and other parts may have such a formidable growth of reeds, that bank fishing is impossible. On the other hand, one can find firm shores with quite deep water, and these are often ideal for spinning for pike and perch.

Owing to the vastness of such loughs as Conn and Cullin, Mask and Corrib, much of the coarse fishing is performed from boats. In this way, likely bays and the waters along the shore line can be explored with greater facility. The emphasis is upon

pike and perch fishing, and it is perhaps true to say that bream
and rudd fishing is still very much in its infancy, although
shoals of both these species of fish swim in vast numbers in the
western lakes. In certain waters pike and perch have been removed in great numbers to improve the trout fishing, but in the
larger lakes a fair stock of both fish must still exist. Here, there
is unlimited scope for the angler, but it is necessary for him
to think on a wide scale. There are various centres in this
part of Ireland, and Crossmolina, Cornamona, Cong, Ough-
terard, Headford, Galway, Tulla, Ennis and Corofin will provide accommodation for the angler, who has a yearning to go
west. There are several lakes on the western side of Lough Corrib
which contain coarse fish, and the attractive lakes around
Corofin are well known for the fishing they provide. Lough
Nafooey situated to the south-west of Lough Mask deserves
special mention. This lough, drained by the River Finny and
enclosed by hills, which rise sharply from its shores, is best
known for the pike it has nurtured and offered to the visiting
angler through the years. Many fine trout have also been taken
from its waters, but the coarse fisherman may note that there
are very good bream there. It is something of a lonely lough,
with its local cattle sometimes standing motionless in the shallow
water on its northern side, and its waters quietly wafted by the
western breeze; but during the year, many anglers make their
way to this most fascinating of Irish loughs, and none doubts
that it has a lure of its own, quite apart from its great pike and
the other fish that swim in its depths.

The Westmeath lakes mainly owe their popularity to their
trout, and the mayfly hatch brings an annual pilgrimage to this
part of Ireland. In more recent time, the various lakes scattered
about Mullingar have attracted the coarse fisherman and much
good sport is available. The principal waters are Loughs Ennell
and Owel, which hold good coarse fish, as do several smaller
loughs nearby. Good coarse fishing used to be available at
Lough Derravaragh, but this oddly shaped water, which is
controlled by the Inland Fisheries Trust, has had many of its

pike and other coarse fish removed in the interest of trout fishing. Lough Lene, just to the east of Derravaragh, contains coarse fish, as does nearby Lough Bane, and these two waters are convenient to Castlepollard. Also within this area are Loughs Iron and Glen. They hold coarse fish, but the former lough is difficult to fish from the bank owing to the fact that it is situated in low-lying land, and its banks are rather heavily reeded.

Lough Sheelin, a section of which lies in County Westmeath, has, like Lough Derravaragh, and for the same reason, been relieved of some of its coarse fish, but it is still a fine pike water. Loughs Kinale and Bracklagh near the village of Finea, also hold pike and other coarse fish, but both these waters are reed infested and are best fished from a boat. Tench are to be found in these two waters, the Dysart lakes near Delvin, and the private lake at Reynella which is owned by well known angler and writer, John Roberts. This lake contains carp as does the small lake of Ballinderry which is situated to the north-east of the village of Moate. At the time of writing, however, it is reported that drainage operations have rendered this water unsuitable for fishing.

The Royal Canal which creeps across the Irish countryside from Clondara in County Longford, passes through Mullingar on its journey eastwards, and this is another feature of the Westmeath district. It contains the usual common species of Irish coarse fish and also tench, and is thus capable of providing an interesting alternative to lough fishing. I would add that the beauty of Lough Sheelin is, in itself, well worth a visit to this part of Ireland, but the angler who is solely interested in results, as often as not finds that his journey there has not been in vain.

The River Blackwater has been especially referred to in the previous chapter as a unique Irish waterway, owing to the fact that it holds two species of fish which are something of a rarity in this country. Another odd feature is that whereas roach, and dace in particular, can be caught in great numbers, there are

no bream, although pike, perch, gudgeon and eels are present.
I once watched a shoal of dace glide up a tributary of the River
Blackwater, passing over two trout resting on the bed of gravel,
and there were so many in the shoal that it was impossible to
estimate their numbers. I have also seen them breaking the surface after fly on a warm June evening, with great frequency.
Suffice to say that more than a few anglers would, I am sure, be
prepared to confirm that a visit to Fermoy, Mallow or Cappoquin can be most rewarding.

Just as the River Blackwater caters for anglers who seek
coarse fishing in the south of Ireland, so is the River Barrow
the centre of coarse fishing activity in the south-east. The river
was made navigable about a century and a half ago, and along
certain stretches of its course, canals were constructed. Sometimes river and canal run side by side and weirs have been
built to maintain an adequate water level in the latter.

As with the Shannon River system, there is no longer any
barge traffic, but the occasional houseboat may be seen passing
through the locks situated along its course. In view of the increase in popularity of cruising holidays in Ireland, there is
every possibility of the River Barrow rivalling the River Shannon as a holiday cruise waterway in future time. Such towns as
Carlow, Bagenalstown and Graignamanagh may once more
find river craft arriving regularly at their deserted quays, and
doubtless this would cause a certain amount of reminiscing,
particularly among the older townsfolk.

The presence of a tow-path or "line" as it is generally known,
guarantees ample bank fishing and because of the alternating
stretches of sluggish and free-running waters, angling need
never lack variety. The river also flows through some of the most
beautiful countryside in Ireland, for its banks are heavily
forested in places, while elsewhere there are deep gorges, lush
water meadows and sometimes there is the atmosphere of the
mill-stream.

The Barrow is best known for its salmon fishing and certain
sections are rigidly preserved and there is also excellent trout

A mixed bag of bream and rudd from Lough Forbes, County Longford

fishing to be had. However, its reputation for being basically a game river, has come about mainly because it was among the last of the main Irish waterways to be "discovered" from a coarse fishing point of view and only the towns of Carlow and Graignamanagh have entertained visiting coarse fishermen to any extent.

Like the Munster Blackwater, it is extensively tidal and a generous proportion of its coarse fish are found in its tidal reaches. Professional salmon fishermen have taken bream and other species of coarse fish in their nets and many a bream has been hooked in the back by a Devon Minnow or other spinner through "trespassing" in salmon pool or trout glide. Its bream shoals tend to be rather scattered, although there are many good quality fish, and there is also a good head of rudd. In those sections where rudd predominate, it is nothing unusual to encounter rudd-bream hybrids and they are very sporting fish.

I have already indicated that the River Barrow contains a large number of pike and perch and in view of my general remarks elsewhere concerning the latter species. I must point out that it is one of the better class Irish perch rivers.

Much of the pike fishing is performed on this river from boats on the even flowing stretches of water, but some really excellent fish have been taken on artificial lures and more particularly dead bait from below weirs or in wide pools, glides which are sometimes divided by thin strips or punctuated by groups of upright reed, and from those areas where the river forms two or more channels, which produce islets and waters with varying currents. In the main small pike alone brave the most powerful current, but big pike are sometimes thereabouts, having found a suitable lair just in the main flow or in the reeds.

I recall disturbing a good pike once, which had been lying in such a spot as this. My angling colleague was some little distance behind me upstream, and on the assumption that the fish would be no more than annoyed by my presence, and had sunk to the river bed a short distance from the bank, I stood still and called out the necessary information to my colleague. He

D

made an accurate cast downstream and promptly hooked the fish. There is a supplementary story to relate concerning this incident, for my colleague had been so distracted by the suddenness of the occurrence, that he had forgotten to give the usual steady strike and the pike dislodged the hooks on rolling over as it was being brought to the bank.

Ireland indeed, has a variety of venues. From the beautiful loughs of Key and Muckno to the mysterious and inviting Nafooey, and from the mighty waters of the River Shannon to the gentle River Rinn. Somewhere along the bank of a river or the shore of a lough an angler may find his Utopia or feel the resistance of a new record fish, and Ireland is just the country to provide such discoveries and experiences.

Chapter Four

ANGLING FOR PIKE

I DO NOT THINK that the Irish pike is especially cunning or shows unusual restraint. It is, however, used to a full and happy life, as it were. Its waters are invariably those of the rich bream, perch and rudd shoals, and such waters are often extensive and remote. When they feed they are ruthless and powerful, but when their appetites are satiated, they are docile and wholly fastidious, even when the opportunity to snap at an attractive lure arises. The smaller pike is more active over a greater period and such fish, even under 1 lb. in weight, will attack the heaviest of spoons and the largest of plugs. It is perhaps discouraging to consider that your bait can pass within inches of a specimen pike, but nothing comes of it because the fish is contentedly digesting a number of other fish, and has, therefore, no interest in the lure, although it is well aware of its presence. There is thus an element of good fortune in the capture of the larger pike, for one has not only to locate its lair, but be there, or within the vicinity thereof, when the fish is feeding. One often finds that such a fish already has a certain number of recently acquired fish in its stomach, and it may be that one's bait was intended to be the last course! The fact that there are always a number of pike which are not taking because their hunting activities have, for the time being, come to an end, prompts one to suggest that the best method of fishing for them would be from a moving boat in order that one can cover the greatest amount of water. On the other hand, one may argue that in every pike water there should be one or two good fish feeding in any given area, and it is more prudent to carefully fish one selected spot.

During my earlier visits to Ireland, I spent far too much time rather aimlessly live baiting in "likely" places. As I have said before, there are a multitude of loughs, and particularly in the Central Plain, with abundant vegetation around their shores and in the shallow bays. In consequence of this, there is often an embarrassment of potential pike holts and all too often the wrong spot can be chosen.

Nowadays, I only use a live fish as bait if I am aware of the presence of a certain pike, or am almost sure that pike are about because of precedent or experience. Last but by no means least, I wish to feel that there is justification for its use as opposed to other methods. I also believe that live baiting is not an act to be reserved for the latter part of the season.

Now let me illustrate some of these remarks. There is a place on one of Ireland's rivers where I have often encountered rudd. Just downstream there is a backwater, and a little farther beyond it there is a bridge. When rudd are active they attract pike from the environs of the bridge and the latter swim up through waters which are ordinarily no more than four feet deep. When my friends and I have been concentrating on the rudd, one of us has slipped away and a live bait has been cast into these shallow waters and a sizeable pike landed. They slip out of the backwater, or move up from or even through the nearest arches of the bridge to prey on the rudd shoals, and the situation calls for the use of a lively fish swimming in the open shallow water above the arches, ready to attract the moving pike.

I have fished there during every month from June to October and none of the pike caught has been under 6 lb. in weight. I am not trying to indicate that upon the first splash of a playful rudd, a multitude of pike awake and come forth from all directions like punters converging on Aintree on Grand National Day. The position is not as dramatic as that, but it is, nevertheless, real enough for a cruising rudd to cross sometimes the path of Esox and it is therefore angling with a purpose.

I would not deny that when live baiting for pike on some

calm, picturesque lough, a patient angler can derive pleasure from the peaceful scene and from observing the sun's rays as they occasionally seek out the paintwork on the upper portion of the float and cause it to stand out above the dark waters, but I am only too aware of the fact that the aggregate number of hours I have spent thus, have been out of all proportion to the number of pike caught. I also believe that some could have been taken by other methods and far more expeditiously.

Although cases have been recorded of two large pike being taken from the same spot or thereabouts and within a short period of time, such incidents are somewhat rare, assuming that by "large pike", one is thinking in terms of 25-pounders or 30-pounders. On the other hand, there is little doubt that waters possessing a good head of large bream, rudd or perch, produce large pike, if Esox is present and this is invariably the case in Ireland.

We know, therefore, that save in those lakes where pike have been removed in large numbers, there is always a reasonable chance of taking at least one pike over, say, the 10-pound mark, without its position being known beforehand. Pike over 25 lb. in weight are not caught "at the drop of a hat", as I have explained elsewhere, although catches of say ten or more pike each weighing up to 5 lb. are made frequently.

How then does the size of the live bait one uses affect one's chances of taking pike? Large pike do not specialise in attacking large fish and the theory of "a big bait for a big fish" has come about, because Jack pike may be reluctant to accept larger baits, or, to put it another way, big pike can tackle large baits more easily. When one has pushed a boat on several occasions through long, wide, thick beds of water lilies and other plants on some of the small loughs, one will have a general idea of the numbers of Jack pike inhabiting them, through watching them leaving their lairs in disgust.

It may be too ambitious an act for one to arrange for a plump rudd or other sizeable live bait to patrol the perimeter of such weed beds, wherein lie these large communities of small pike,

each quietly fanning its tail beneath a selected lily pad, for it
may be found that no pike is prepared to accept the lure, or if
one does, that it makes a false run, in that it grabs and carries
off the bait as best it can, and then either releases it or goes to
the bottom without making any attempt to swallow it.

Once when fishing the clear waters of a County Leitrim
lough, I was able to observe a small pike do precisely this. It
lay on the bed facing me for fully five minutes with the bait
between its jaws before releasing it. Such actions also indicate
an element of greed on the part of pike, in that live baits may be
taken because they are conveniently available, although the
fish concerned may have previously satisfied their appetites.

Tales which illustrate the savagery of pike and their gluttony
are very common, but I prefer to take a broad view of them and
regulate the size of the live baits I use, according to my needs.

The largest natural bait I ever used was a $2\frac{1}{2}$ lb. pike, which
was launched from a boat fairly near to a spot where a very
large pike had been seen. It was never taken and shortly after
it was eventually withdrawn, a colleague cast a spoon bait into
the same area of water and hooked, rather ironically I thought,
a pike rather larger than the one I had been using as a live bait.

I have spent many a pleasant hour on small Irish rivers
where pike were plentiful, using a small live fish as bait, which
had been hooked through the upper lip and allowed to drift
downstream, guided by a cork-bodied float. This is a very active
method of live baiting and I normally reserve its use for the
exploration of small rivers such as the Rinn and the Little
Brosna and the upper sections of large rivers.

When lough fishing or angling on the quieter stretches of
large rivers or at pools along their courses, I often use a dead
bait if I have decided to use a natural as opposed to an artificial
bait. I have two plans of campaign in readiness and the em-
ployment of each depends on the water depth. The more frequently used one, which has enabled one of my colleagues and
myself to take more pike than by any other method save for
trolling, is the "sink and draw" method, whereby a small rudd

or perch is threaded with trace wire through vent and mouth, and a large, single hook is then attached to the trace and pulled into the side of the mouth.

I have made previous reference to this style of angling, but here I should mention that no harm will be done by knotting both the fish and the trace at the tail with silk or strong cotton. There is no need to dispose of unused dead baits, but they must be kept in a cool place. I have used perch and rudd forty-eight hours after capture and they have been taken without apparent concern by pike and also perch and trout for that matter.

Many pike have been taken by this method, and if the peri-meter of a lough is reasonably traversable, the opportunity should be taken of angling thus. The other method is just as simple to use although it was never designed for anglers with weak hearts! I refer to dead bait surface fishing where a small fish, preferably a rudd or "silver" bream, is secured by a single hook through both lips and quietly cast into shallow bays and backwaters, or river pools where there is no pronounced current.

In this present age there may be too much emphasis laid on modern tackle and too little on natural fishing. There is no great difference between a pike claiming one of a shoal of rudd lying near to the surface and one attacking a solitary fish float-ing on the water surface. In 1952 I watched an Irish pike fisherman carefully coil line from his ancient centre-pin reel on to the bank and then cast a lip-hooked rudd with a sturdy two-piece rod into a river pool about five feet deep, with a carpet of weed and a few clusters of waving underwater reeds thereabouts. Having done this, he reeled in the superfluous line, sat down and lit his pipe. In due course, a pike flashed through the light green water and shattered the silence of the evening as it seized the bait, almost wholly exposing itself as it did so. The angler eyed the situation unperturbed. He drew on his pipe, perhaps half a dozen times and then, after quietly winding in the loose line, he struck.

I can readily recall the scene because it was a quiet, peaceful, splendorous, late September evening, and doubtless I could have

performed the act more fairly and easily with my modern spinning rod and fixed-spool reel, but certainly not more thoroughly
or knowledgeably. It is a style which is ideal for shaking the pike
out of its solemnity as it lies in its watery den, and one which
should be given greater attention.

Turning to the subject of spinning, sometimes the perpetual
"plop plop" of silver spoons sounds like a spring shower on a
popular lough. The spinning rod can be a deadly weapon in
more than one sense and I remember many years ago a colleague trying out my then new Hardex reel and casting a lure
over one of the River Shannon's highest bridges without any
difficulty whatsoever. The act of retrieving it was not as simple!
It is the weapon of the hunter, but one must know where to hunt
and what is more important, how to hunt, to be even fairly
successful. I have made, elsewhere, references to the possible
lairs of pike and any further comments here would be superfluous, but it is perhaps worth mentioning that the spinning
enthusiast may only give scant attention to, or perhaps not even
consider, the position from the point of view of location, but
rely on what I can only describe as the "average basis" of
angling; that is to say he may decide to fish a lough, the peri-
meter of which he can conveniently cover during the time he has
at his disposal, or perhaps cover a section thereof twice.

Certain anglers simply tackle up at the part of the lough they
reach first, and commence to spin away at convenient spots
until their enthusiasm wanes, the elements turn against them,
their desire for nourishment emulates that of the local pike
population, or it becomes time to depart. This approach does
little to increase one's knowledge of the habits of pike and its
main contribution to angling in general has been to coin a new
phrase, or rather give a new interpretation to an old one,
namely "go for a spin". I must admit that my angling friends
and I have all been guilty of this peripatetic, itinerant, nomadic
approach to the subject, but I now consider the use of the artificial lure as carefully as I do the live bait.

Results have been reasonably fair throughout the years for

myself and my colleagues. I would not say more than that. Knowledgeable Irish anglers may well tell you to seek out your copper spoon and subdue it with moist gravel. The colour is just right, they say. If you ignore their advice and catch nothing, as sure as the sun sets on Galway Bay, one of the sages will cross your path later on, carrying a 15-pounder and there will be a "I told you so" look on his face.

I have a liking for copper, silver, golden or red spoons and if I think the quarry can see them I am content. Should the converse be the position, I think in terms of sound as well as colour and fish a bright type of bar-spoon.

Clear, open shores give little or no guide to the whereabouts of pike and yet they are often there, usually on the lookout for perch or other fish. Much depends on the composition of the bed and the physical construction of the lough about the shore line.

It must never be assumed that shallow water holds no joy for the pike angler any more than that deep water right up to the very edge of the loughside will generally provide the best fishing. I do not think there is any short cut to success once the extreme shallows and stretches of water lying over bare rock have been eliminated from a list of potential fishing grounds. The gradually deepening water with a bed of sand or gravel and patches of underwater vegetation, and the even type of lough bed of silt or clay, with its carpet of weeds are the two kinds of water that one encounters most frequently.

Occasionally one finds water of great depth and it is arguable whether one can reasonably expect to find fish of any species frequenting the proximity of the bed, let alone pike, and particularly during the first months of the coarse fishing season, when the temperature never drops low enough to cause any serious water disturbance. However, the pike angler does not find himself having to consider, prove, or disprove this point very often.

Reverting to the lesser deeps and the use of artificial lures, I think it wise to formulate a plan of action and adhere to it.

A colleague and I have spent many days spinning for pike and we have adopted a practice which has produced some good pike while retaining our individuality. We would decide on an area where we would concentrate our activities, but we would not commence fishing independently at either extremity of the water. There was an implied agreement between us that we would start by using the same type of lure, but there would be a variation in the colour scheme. There was no question of deciding who should fish above the other. Whoever was ready first would walk a reasonable distance along the shore and start from a certain point. If the water was of fair depth we would each use a spoon or bar-spoon, and we employed the bait in whatever manner we preferred. As a result of performing various actions with rod-top and reel, a bait can be made to do most things, and we each have our own ideas on the subject. If practicable, I tend to engage a bait in a quiet series of vertical "V" movements, right from the moment the bait touches the water.

Upon reaching shallower water we would continue to use the same lures, although it was necessary to retrieve them more quickly, and whereas there was a decided bias on the part of small pike to attack them, it was always possible that an aroused, hungry or annoyed adult pike might be hooked and so we would fish in this manner for a short while before changing to plug bait.

Whoever was in the van would then return to the beginning of the shallows and start to follow the other party, using a plug of a different colour.

As perch are so widespread in Ireland, red has been one of our favourite colours through the years, and the green coloured plug is undoubtedly the most enigmatic. I have such a plug which has been "plundered" by pike, and the teeth marks thereon provide ample evidence of this. The effect this bait has on pike however, can be wholly innocuous on occasions, while others attract.

When we had covered the water, we would relax, meditate and discuss any worthwhile matters such as fish which had been aroused or moved. It was an easy enough task to mark the point of encounter with a stone or two, if there were no obvious natural characteristics available. Such acts would suggest that it was our intention to cover once more the water we have just fished, and this was precisely what we used to do.

Our method of fishing these open shores is probably not rare, but neither, I suspect, is it commonplace. We expect to catch fish on the return journey if signs have been promising and we may even achieve better results. At the least we find we are fishing the water thoroughly, and I think that there is much to be said for a concentration of effort thus.

This method can provide interesting experiences. On one occasion I found myself taking perch after perch on a red and silver spoon; I think about seventeen in all. My colleague, following me, caught nine pike on a plain, silver spoon. The water was none too clear and the sky overcast. I recall that this raised some interesting issues between us about the respective powers of vision of these two species of fish and I also recall that when I recommenced fishing, I forgot about theory and produced an all-silver spoon and started to catch pike.

I have often wondered just how thorough one can be in the noble (some say scientific) act of lough shore spinning, but interesting events are always likely to occur in Ireland and I remember one unprecedented occasion when I cast a spoon into the centre of a small bay and hooked a pike fairly and squarely on the snout! It did not know what had hit it, as they say, and for a moment or so, I was equally unsure what I had hit!

And now a final word about Irish rivers and their pike. On the wide sections of such rivers as the Shannon, Suck and Corrib, most of my piking activities have been conducted from a boat, as previously mentioned. There are many rivers where one can confidently go forth and tread the bank in search of pike, but all too often the main rivers are anything but intimate, and sometimes there is such a heavy weed growth that this form of angling is out of the question. Then, only the boat can enable the angler to seek his goal and if he is reluctant to take to the water, then he had best forget about pike fishing.

Ironically enough, once an angler is converted to boat fishing, he may well neglect the river bank and only rarely find
himself fishing waters unsuited to boat fishing but which possess pike. Such waters may be divided into two categories,
namely those where river currents are varied because of the
presence of weirs, islets, subsidiary streams, irregular weed
formations and the like, and those of the steadily flowing, often
meandering river, where one can easily cast to the opposite
bank.

Concerning the former, they inevitably provide excellent pike
fishing because their aerated waters are favoured by trout, if
they frequent the river concerned, and in Ireland there is every
chance of this, and also by perch shoals, possibly because of the
presence of mossy stones and gravel, and in times of drought it
is very likely that other species of fish will be drawn to them.

They are thus favoured by pike, a fact well known to the
young, local angler, who may be seen at such places, casting
a perch into the waters, using a large cork as a float, in the hope
that Esox will accept the morsel. It is well worth ignoring tradition, and to allow a plug to flutter and dance in and around the
eddies and permit a spoon to rise and fall and be jerked in the
current. I have long since failed to register surprise when a pike
has been taken from such waters, as opposed to the quieter areas
usually found at the side of the river.

Pike will take up position there as long as there is something
solid and stable for them to lurk behind, and which enables
them to remain without expending too much energy. I once
came across a pool just above a small weir on the upper section
of the River Erne. I cast a spoon into it and a pike took it
immediately, and two more pike followed in quick succession.

On another occasion a friend and I took fifteen pike from a
short stretch of water below a weir. Clumps of reeds were scattered about the water and I got the impression that there was a
pike's head protruding from each clump, a little below the
water surface. They found the passing spoon bait quite irresis-

tible and even a one-eyed pike of about 12 lb. fell to the lure. I understand that a 15 lb. trout was taken from this stretch of water some years ago and I am surprised it lived long enough to attain that weight!

As occasion demands I endeavour to emulate the feats of the aforementioned gossoons and search the water with dead bait. My previous references to dead bait fishing for pike have been mainly in connection with trolling, or angling in still water, and the methods I have described for attaching the bait to the trace are simple and effective, but they will not necessarily suffice in more turbulent waters.

I do not go to the other extreme and festoon the bait with hooks or, indeed, mount it. I attach a treble to one end of the trace, then slip the trace through the eye of a second treble hook. The former is attached to the fish's tail and the latter just past the gill cover, having wound the trace four or five times round the shank of the second treble. The free end of the trace is then passed through the gill cover and out of the mouth of the bait and is attached to the line by means of a swivel. It is necessary to ensure that the swim-bladder of the fish has been punctured and lead may have to be added to the line to sink the bait. Perhaps I should add that a dead rudd floats well and if one is surface fishing, it is equally important to refrain from bursting the swim-bladder.

I do not wish to give the impression that pike are readily caught from "broken water" or where the stream is like a mill race, although I would not pretend that this can never be. I very well remember a pike, and a large one at that, desperately flinging itself out of the water in an endeavour to reach a lure I was obliged to retrieve rather quickly during the final stages of withdrawal when salmon fishing. I have also taken pike when spinning for trout in what is generally termed "fast water". A colleague took a hen pike of about 17 lb. also when salmon fishing, and the fish caused the line to decapitate a row of rushes during its powerful fight for freedom.

These are the less usual types of incidents that arise and long may they do so to remind the angler of the uncertainty of angling, but my main intention is to infer that more pike are capable of being taken from the steady stream, as opposed to the quiet edges and back flows than may be imagined.

I would now turn to the subject of trolling which is one quite foreign to many anglers visiting Ireland and certain routine acts may need to be learned. Anglers who have no experience of casting from a boat while seated, might find that they despatch the bait with too high a trajectory or move the rod horizontally through too wide an arc, thus causing the bait to either fall short, or to hit the water on the wrong side of the boat's wake.

It is easier to cast standing up, but if one happens to lose one's balance, fishing may be over for the day or even longer! Experienced trollers rarely follow this practice and it is not difficult to master the back-hand cast. Oarsmen tend to register an expression of concern on their countenances when a bait hovers about them prior to casting, but they get used to it!

It is the practice of certain anglers to set down their rod after casting and some boats have a special rest fitted to hold it, the butt being placed on the near side of one of the boat's ribs. If one is trolling alone, it is essential to wedge the rod thus, or secure it in some other way, but with a colleague at the oars, it is to one's advantage to hold the rod.

I once saw a rod pulled over the side of a boat by a large pike and had the owner not possessed unusually long arms, a few pounds worth of tackle would probably have been lost. As it was, the fish freed itself quite easily because of the slackness in the line and it was one well worth catching.

I keep hold of the rod for various reasons. With practice one learns to gauge the approximate depth of the water over which one is trolling by the amount of pressure exerted on the rod, and in addition, the slightest interference with the bait can usually be detected, although on one or two occasions when fishing a river, I have known small perch to become attached to a lure without announcing their presence.

A short, steady resistance may well mean that weeds have fouled the hook or a minor "knock" may indicate that the lure has passed through a clump of weeds. It could also mean that the hooks have become entangled with the trace through inter-ference of some nature. In such cases the lure should be in-spected and any necessary action taken.

That then is what one might term the practical side to trol-ling, and the next stages of the subject are when and where to pursue predatory fish. As I have made certain references to the likely haunts of pike and perch elsewhere, I propose to review these subjects from the point of view of climatic conditions and the manner in which they can affect the feeding habits and movement of these fish through the year.

There is a definite tendency for pike, for example, to curb their normal feeding habits through the presence of much fresh water as a result of continuous, heavy rainfall, which raises the levels of loughs and rivers a considerable distance above their normal water-lines.

Heavy rainfall, however, can have the opposite effect for a limited period after drought conditions, because of the bene-ficial increase in the oxygen content of the waters concerned. Days of bright periods and occasional showers with westerly or southerly breezes are foremost in my mind when I think of "piking weather". These conditions harmonise and keep feed-ing pike in search of prey. Bright, breezy days are also to be recommended, with the wind blowing across lough or down the river valley, stirring up the surface and cooling the water, although away from lough or river one may be forgiven for be-ing dubious about any possible success.

Periods of calm with descending or ascending temperatures cannot be considered so confidently. Pike take their time adjusting themselves, and existing weather conditions mean little. The most frequently quoted reference in this respect is to those mild spells during the winter months when nature deigns to treat one to a few days of pleasant calm. It is presumptuous of one to spin the lure or cast the natural bait prematurely, and the all-season angler must bide his time and wait for the day when pike are finally aroused and "Jack" become active in the shallows and may be caught in numbers.

Periods of summer calm are observed by a far greater number of anglers, and whether the days concerned be overshadowed by low cloud ceilings which only threaten but never swell lough or river, or confirm that a ridge of high pressure is surprisingly stationary, I have learned to view them with some apprehension, particularly in relation to lough fishing.

These periods of hot, calm weather need little explanation; listlessness or relaxation are the operative words so far as pike are concerned, especially during the main part of the day. Gloomy, overcast conditions are more difficult to examine and yet I have found pike lethargic as a result of them, whether I have been concentrating my efforts on some tiny lough or some more imposing piece of water.

Inevitably, the beginning of such a spell of weather provides the best fishing, for as the days progress pike become more and more reluctant to feed. When, however, the settled weather changes, it is sometimes found that fish are being caught "unexpectedly", or alternatively that certain anglers are registering disappointment because they are not getting satisfactory results during what they deem to be favourable conditions.

As an example of this, I recall one very hot day in September, when a pleasant sit down in a deckchair would have been more in keeping with the weather. After a week of excellent pike fishing under broken skies and with occasional showers and fair breezes, the weather suddenly changed, in tourist jargon "for the better". The lough in question and adjoining river were becalmed and wasps and gnats were present everywhere.

My friends and I continued to troll for pike and during the day we hooked five fish and caught four weighing 4 lb., 5 lb., $7\frac{1}{2}$ lb. and 15 lb., and the other fish which freed itself by diving under a partly submerged bush, was again in double figures.

As a complete contrast, however, I recall that on another day in September some years before (in 1954), after several weeks

The Author with a sizeable bream taken from the River Shannon at Rooskey, County Leitrim

of rain, there was a refreshing break between in-moving troughs of low pressure and there was just one day of blue skies and absolute calm. I spent the whole of that day in the giant bulb of water at the southern end of Lough Corrib. The volume of fresh water in the lough had already had its effect on the pike there, and although we skirted around the edges of some of the smaller islands which were completely submerged, and passed what remained of certain weed beds, we caught but one small pike, though as a consolation prize an excellent brown trout of, I think, 5 lb. 5 oz. fell to a copper spoon. The position was much the same at other loughs in the area, which were all boasting new shore lines while the floods persisted.

When the water level is normal during calm spells, I think one's best chances are to be had during the last couple of hours of daylight and also during the late afternoon, so far as the latter months of the year are concerned.

No doubt pike enjoy the coolness of evenings that follow warm days, when no "stirring-up" of the water had occurred, but it is always doubtful whether they are prepared to feed with that keenness one normally associated with them, and as I have mentioned elsewhere, one may be far better off pursuing other species of fish.

The final subject upon which I intend to reflect is water depth, although the angler will not be concerned with this matter too frequently, because of the comparative shallowness of many of the smaller Irish loughs. Firstly, it is necessary to differentiate between summer and winter conditions. Between, say, November and the end of February many pike are to be found in the deepest water available in loughs, because water temperature is often at its highest point about the beds of loughs and because many of the fish upon which pike prey, have also made for such places for the same reason.

In consequence of this, it is reasonable to assume that trolling operations should be concentrated on those areas of loughs where the water is at its deepest, but it must not be forgotten that all pike do not desert their lairs and as hunger demands,

E

continue to search for those perch shoals which, like their predatory colleagues, still inhabit the lough fringes and bays.

Certainly during periods of very cold weather, it is just as
unlikely that the depths are going to produce more pike in
taking mood than other regions, and the probability is that no
records will be broken anywhere. During mild spells I feel
that one may well see more action in the shallows.

It is during the summer months and in early autumn that
the deep sections of loughs have more to offer. Perhaps at this
point I ought to mention that I consider any water over twenty-
five feet deep to fall into this category. I have trolled across
water three times that depth and more, and although such water
would barely accommodate an inverted cricket pitch, it is truly
deep water trolling by Irish standards.

It is worth while seeking out areas of deep water once the
coarse fishing season is under way, but I would repeat that once
a warm spell has arrived or other adverse conditions prevail as
aforementioned, it is likely that pike will not be found in
too active a mood and especially during the main part of the
day.

My records and my memory remind me that investigation of
these waters during such conditions have produced little result,
but on the other hand, it is sometimes worth while to venture
out during the cool of the evening and also when the weather
can be described as "bright and breezy" or changeable, and
trail a lure in twenty to forty feet of water.

Each incident involving a successful hooking of a fish, tends
to stand out in one's mind, because of the eeriness of coming
into contact with a fish many feet below the surface. The
"knocks" on the rod top seem more prolonged, and visual
contact and the feeling that one really has control over the
fish, tend to come about unhurriedly.

On occasion I have had these deep stretches of water or
deep runs or trenches pointed out to me by experienced local
anglers and have seen the boat manoeuvred carefully into position, so that the bait could be trailed along their courses, and I

have known the boat to be stopped and a lure cast into and drawn quietly out of craters on the lough bed, which were recognised haunts of pike, too small in area to investigate other than by "trolling" in the official sense of the word.

What is it then that causes me to believe that areas of deep water provide better pike fishing during the summer than in winter? The main reason is that pike will frequent them for the purpose of feeding during the summer and that the angler catches them there, because then he is more likely to find them active. In other words, they go there by choice, and a combination of reduced temperature down below, together with a freshening of the surface water by wind, renders them active, as is the case with a general lowering of the temperature during the evening, although the wind may have abated or dropped completely.

During the winter, pike are there usually through necessity and are frequently torpid and thus disinclined to feed, and cold winds hardly improve matters.

One may expect too much of really deep water, for the feeling of confident anticipation conjured up by the excitement of fishing many feet below in a mysterious and uncharted world wherein monster pike dwell, is a very natural one.

However, the bed may consist of hard, uninteresting rock, or it may be the resting place of waste matter, disliked by fish. Concerning water temperature, it is often apparent that fish have little desire to frequent this section of a lough, and if those species upon which pike prey are absent, Esox will be absent too. It is also most unusual to find water plants growing at depths exceeding, say, ten feet.

Stories are fairly common about anglers who have hooked "something big" down below, and after having been towed across the lough for some time, have cut the line through tedium or indeed apprehension because of the proximity of rocks or rising winds.

As a matter of fact, an angler who persists in using line with a breaking strain of say, 20 lb. and who finds himself on a lough in a dinghy or some flat-bottomed craft, is liable to be towed around by even a 10 lb. pike with the utmost facility.

To my way of thinking, trolling is not a way of spending a few hours angling without effort, or an act which gives one the opportunity to relax from the more serious business of bank fishing and simulate the mood of visitors to Scotland who decide to spend an afternoon on the Clyde.

I view it in an equal light to bank fishing, whether at a swim to which I have committed myself, or whether spinning therefrom for predators, and look upon it as an interesting, and provided the right tackle is used, a fair style of angling. Whatever one may think of its merits, however, it has to be agreed that it gives one an excellent opportunity of getting to grips with offshore pike and it is a time-honoured part of Irish coarse fishing.

Chapter Five

ANGLING FOR PERCH

THE MOST LIKELY FISH to be found by observation are rudd, and bream the most likely by design, for one sees more of the leaping of the rudd than the rolling of bream or the presence of bubbles that the latter have created. It would seem that the larger head of specimen pike are to be found in the great lakes and also the River Shannon and its principal tributaries, but big perch can be difficult to find, although I fancy that there are more in the general run of Irish waters than may be imagined. When rivers are in spate and much of the weed growth has died and fry are clinging to the edges, the prowling perch must often be in close proximity, but the majority of visiting anglers have already left by then and local anglers are scarce. Similarly, there are more deep holes in loughs harbouring good perch than there are ever anglers to explore them.

During the latter part of the year I have usually found myself in areas where perch fishing was not one of the more prominent talking points among anglers, and other pursuits have been the order of the day. There have been days, however, when I have searched for big perch in loughs where only small perch are normally caught, and although results have sometimes been encouraging, few fish approaching the specimen class have come to net, as yet.

There are several places I should like to visit or re-visit during late autumn or winter, as for example Lough Gowna, and particularly the area near to the village of that name, and also the Ballymote district, and certain of the smaller loughs north of Galway. There are also waters on the western section of the border between Eire and Northern Ireland where good catches of perch have been recorded. Location is the obvious problem concerning the big loughs, but during the autumn I have had some success when long-distance legering at carefully chosen spots in certain of the meandering bays of Lough Corrib, and this more subtle type of angling has provided a sharp contrast to the carefree act of thinning out shoals of the smaller perch found in such waters.

My colleagues and I have caught quite large perch when spinning waters where the weight of perch was above average, and we have also caught such fish when on the troll, and again when legering or even float-fishing in "big perch" waters. Several of them have been taken when angling for other fish, and by that I mean not only pike and bream but also rudd. In fact, one of the biggest perch I have caught in Ireland was taken on redworm, when fishing slightly away from a rudd shoal after moving the float a couple of feet up the line. I also recall that on finding a rudd shoal being most active about the surface, I caught a sizeable perch by drawing a spinner through the tail of the shoal. Another perch of similar size was also taken, and it is worth recording that the playing and capture of the perch did not bother the shoal, for it retained its general position in the river and the rudd continued to feed enthusiastically when I recommenced angling for them.

One of the best day's perch fishing I ever experienced occurred when trolling on a County Leitrim lough. It was a dark, dismal day and the wind was blowing strongly up the lough. The previous day my companion and I had caught several small perch from a nearby canal and they were used as bait, a wire trace being threaded through vent and mouth, with a single hook drawn into the side of the mouth. It is a fact that during certain intervals the boat had hardly started to move off again, after one fish had been caught, before another seized the bait. We had, incidentally, been requested by our hostess to retain a couple of large perch if we met with success, and this we did. She enquired as to whether we liked to eat them and the reply was in the negative, although I hinted, with tongue in cheek, that my wife did. On the following morning my colleague and I were presented with the usual delicious "Irish fry", but with the utmost pride and reverence, one carefully prepared perch was laid before my wife! Sadly, it was of the cotton-wool variety and I have never been allowed to forget that indiscretion of mine!

The best river perch I ever caught accepted a fair portion of one of those long, white worms with an ash-blue tint, which are found in orchards around tree roots. They are really tough worms which can grow to immense proportions and the pity of it is that they are not too readily available. I caught the fish in question while fishing a deep gully under the main current and it put up a fair fight before I was able to land it and discover that it weighed 2 lb. 4 oz.

One of my colleagues once caught a brace of perch an ounce below and above this weight when legering a minnow as bait in a pool below a weir.

Environment has had much to do with our lack of success, but the countless hundreds of small perch we have taken have kept us very active and we have much to be thankful for in this respect.

I have taken some of my best perch from those sections of rivers and loughs where the bed was sandy of stone infested, yet had a certain definite weed growth. When fishing notable perch rivers, I have been fortunate enough to entice some of them from their lairs which have been not so much in deep pools below weirs, or holes beneath trees, as in the faster water thereabouts. I think this is a point well worth remembering. I have also spent pleasant hours perch fishing from a stationary boat on both lough and river, but the boat was used because it was the only means whereby I could reach the desired location, and did not contribute in any other way, as it would for example when trolling for perch and pike, or when seeking rudd visually.

Perch may be easy to locate, but they do not physically betray their presence over-generously. When they do, it is ironically enough all too obviously, but it only really happens in three ways. The first is after the spawning season, when shoals can sometimes be seen simulating rudd, in that they will choose an easy-flowing stretch of water, as for example the inside bend of a river and swim about almost at surface level, with the occasional fish actually breaking surface. They seem to go about this business more thoroughly than do rudd, and sometimes they are so conspicuous that it might be believed they were situated in but a few inches of water.

The second way may occur at any time of the year and I refer to the act of adult perch chasing fry. It is one so well known that I need not comment further, save to add that it is worth while to have a small spinner available when perch act in this way.

The remaining one is only witnessed by the angler who is fortunate enough to be able to fish the larger type of lough when autumn arrives, and results from the migratory habits of perch. I have made scant reference to this subject elsewhere, so I feel I should elaborate a little, for some of the most fascinating angling Ireland has to offer is available on the big loughs at this time of the year.

During the summer perch are generally content to feed in reasonably shallow water around the lough perimeter and rest among the weed beds, or near stones and plant life on the lough bed. The lower stretches of feeder streams are often packed with perch, provided their waters are not too turbulent as a result of the streams descending sharply over the final sections of their courses.

During the latter part of the year when much of the aquatic vegetation has ceased to flourish and when the temperature has dropped to a less kindly number of degrees, many perch seek the deeper water out in the lough. Prior to the commencement of the journey, they congregate in formidable numbers at certain points along the shore line or in bays, and on bright, calm days, and providing the water is clear enough, these large shoals can be seen by the angler. A fly-spoon or small Devon

Minnow is all that is needed to ensure success and one may get tired of the "slaughter" long before the fish do.

So much for the visual side to perch fishing, and as I have reintroduced the subject of spinning, I think the following comments are worth mentioning. Much as the hungry perch seems to have little respect for the size of an artificial lure presented to it, lest it be of gigantic proportions, there is no doubt that the smaller size of lure takes the greatest number of fish.

Too many perch have followed a large bait without taking (and sometimes almost to the feet of the angler in question) for one to say otherwise, and much as they will sometimes tackle baits whose respective sizes are out of all proportion to the size of the perch concerned, I feel that it is generally wise to fish a small lure when spinning for them. One will find that the colour of the water has little effect on perch and that they will respond just as willingly to the vibrations set up by Devon Minnows in rivers which have been coloured by the outflow of water from rain-washed bogland, as they will to the smooth action of a small copper spoon guided by the angler through the clear waters of a limestone lough.

Just as summer roach sometimes appear as if from nowhere in English rivers and take a carefully trotted bait, so Irish perch materialise, as it were, and attack an artificial lure as it is manoeuvred towards the shore. I remember that during one of my first visits to Ireland, I was startled by the joint splashes of a couple of perch which, simultaneously but unsuccessfully attacked the lure I was withdrawing too quickly and too near the surface of the shallow water at the edge of the lough. The lure was but a few feet from me when the incident occurred and at the time I was contemplating where my next cast should be made. The circumstances of the event prompted me to make a similar cast and with the rod held at a less acute angle to the water surface and the bait moving more slowly, one of those perch (I presume) was hooked. Naturally, I searched the water for another fish but met with no success. There is nothing to be lost by fishing a bait right up to one's feet, but few large perch seem to get caught on the last lap, as it were.

Opinions on the feeding activities of perch or other fish for that matter will always be given in relation to the state of the water. Colour causes me far less concern than temperature. The heat of summer can make perch listless and affect their senses, and cause a passing spinner to sound like a jet plane, so swiftly do they flee sometimes, yet they may well attack a minnow! A cold spell can render them morose but during these latter conditions, while they may refuse a natural bait, they may suddenly become agitated at the sight or "feel" of a small spinner.

There are enough cloudy days and pleasant breezes in Ireland during the summer months to prevent one worrying too much about these points and there are sufficient locations and, of course, perch themselves for one to be particularly anxious about where to find them and the number one will catch.

There are many baits associated with perch fishing and I normally use lobworms, small rudd or minnows in conjunction with a running leger and search the water thoroughly, either by taking in line or recasting at regular intervals, for one is seeking individual fish, or perhaps a brace. Unlike the smaller fish, the full bodied mature perch is either a solitary soul or one which may deign to associate with another fish of like proportions, or occasionally a small, adult shoal.

There is a certain section of a lough in County Cavan, where the shore line falls away almost immediately, and one can cast into about ten feet of water, and some farther distance out the depth is nearer forty feet. Excellent perch and also pike have been caught from this shore and I have particularly fond memories of it, for it was there that I experienced a rather unusual event.

I had advised a fellow angler to fish these waters, and one bright and sunny morning he did so. Later in the day I met him and he told me he had caught one very good perch, but had been broken by another. He had been using the familiar pearshaped type of leger and lobworm had been his bait. Afterwards, my colleague and I decided to take out a boat as conditions had become suitable for trolling, and eventually we happened to pass over this part of the lough.

One could feel the steady pressure extended on the spoon bait and rod top, as the former trailed through the deep water, and then the rod quivered excitedly as a fish took the bait. It was played carefully and gradually line was brought in, but then something occurred which caused my colleague and I to exchange glances of disbelief. The spoon had been reeled right out of the water, but there was no fish present, and yet the line was still taut! There, attached to one of the trebles was a loop, and its accompanying line went down beneath the water surface. Fortunately, this alien tackle was of no great length and the fish at the other end was subsequently landed without having to consider how one could possibly arrange for the spoon to pass through the top ring of the trolling rod!

The fish was unhooked and the strangely acquired tackle, which included a pear-shaped leger, was carefully preserved. I have no need to describe the look on the face of its owner when it was eventually returned to him, together with a note of that fish's weight. One important lesson to be learned from this incident is that of ensuring that the knots one uses should be of the recommended type. The loop which had attached itself so amazingly to one of the hooks of my lure in all that volume of water, had no tell-tale portion of line attached to it. Thus if a more secure form of knot had been used, that fish would probably not have been caught "secondhand". It weighed 2 lb. 1 oz. incidentally.

Big perch are powerful and curious, suspicious and un-neighbourly, and they will place discretion before hunger. Occasionally they will pluck at a small bait but they will also savage baits out of all proportion to the size of their mouths. This latter act may be the result of a momentary return to the over-ambitious activities of their youth, or perhaps through annoyance. It is one more normally reserved for big pike, and experience prompts me to say that the trusty lobworm is just about the best bait to employ when searching for this bright-eyed and fastidious adult fish, with its superlative shoulders and careful ways. Anglers will not infrequently encounter a portion of a lough which suggests the presence of good perch and it is sometimes a good thing to forget about rudd and bream and "rummage among the rocky depths" as it were.

I have given much space to the subject of bream location, with particular reference to mud and silt, and as perch have been strongly connected with beds of stone, sand and gravel, and as the two species have a definite leaning towards lobworms and deep water, it may be felt that provided one adheres to these requirements it does not really matter where one elects to fish, for one will have an even chance of locating one or other of the species.

This, unfortunately, is not the simple position that theory tends to infer. Were there as many specimen perch in Ireland as there, undoubtedly, are bream, and if the former goodly fish were scattered over a wide field, the act of perch fishing would be more freely practised than it is. Whereas I feel that perch should be sought after more than they are, there is always the proviso that this act really has to be performed in certain well-defined waters, from the point of view of guaranteeing their presence.

The mighty River Shannon, notwithstanding its teeming millions of coarse fish, is not a recommended perch river, but from investigation I have found half a dozen places where I know there is a fair chance of locating the larger of the species. A certain percentage of each generation of anglers will come across such spots, scattered along the course of this waterway, and some will surely reap the reward of their endeavours, and other anglers, no doubt, are aware of or will find other places which are capable of producing large perch.

Good perch have been recorded from the southern River Blackwater to the imposing Lough Arrow and from the River

Suck to Lough Mask, and with the ever increasing interest being taken in coarse fishing in Ireland, it could be that sometime in the future, a perch which will be subsequently known as "the daddy of them all" will come to net. Although it may be taken on the troll or as a result of spinning from bank or shore, it is probably more likely to accept some form of dainty morsel, gracefully but tantalisingly placed near to its lair, and if the sweetmeat happens to be a gay bunch of brandlings, or more especially a seductive lob from an Irish garden, I shall not be the least bit surprised.

Chapter Six

ANGLING FOR COMMON BREAM

THERE ARE some anglers who look upon bream as being really nothing more than shoaling fish, which when feeding, follow one another surely and almost monotonously to the keepnet.

In Ireland such a confident view cannot be held for various reasons. Quite apart from the state of the weather or the time of the year, the point I first learned to appreciate more than any other about bream, was that as often as not I was angling for fish which had previously only been disturbed by the occasional tread of a farmer's boot, animals which had come to drink at the water's edge, an ambitious predator, or a youth throwing stick or stone, and the bed had only been disturbed by underwater currents, sinking matter and the natural activities of bream themselves.

Even now, in those waters away from the more prominent angling centres, or those rarely fished save from a boat, bream are still unused to groundbait and unfamiliar with certain baits, so that the angler must be prepared to be patient and educate the fish to his way of thinking and style of angling, or alternatively fish in a manner which will neither be suspicious to nor will be met with indifference by these "uncivilised" bream. Two further points which immediately follow are, respectively, the liking bream have for "the pleasant stream" and the difficulty of locating them because of the colour of many waters which flow through or are fringed by bogland, and the fact that they are situated in the open countryside and susceptible to the merest zephyr. Thus, they do not always lend themselves to quiet investigation on the part of the angler who is hoping to perceive visible signs of bream.

There is no guarantee, even when bream are prepared to half expose themselves, that when they feed, they will do so within close proximity to where they have been sighted.

I remember being introduced to a wide pool on one of Ireland's minor rivers and it transpired that as I was actually setting up my tackle, two bream showed themselves in a manner that I have come to look upon as being a pre-feeding act. I carefully searched the water both at the spot and below where they had appeared but without result, and subsequently began to angle for them at the latter spot. No bites were forthcoming so I eventually left the pool and took up a position some yards below the mouth of the outflowing river where the water was comparatively deep. It was there that I found the bream.

The use of groundbait is one of the controversial subjects of angling. I have given some indication elsewhere of when I feel it need not be used or can be over-used in relation to bream fishing, and occasionally I have found myself engaged in friendly arguments with certain of Ireland's own anglers on this matter. I believe that bream have missed capture because it has been used prematurely, but I also believe that many more bream have never had a chance of offering themselves as quarry because it has been ignored by the angler.

Given the time and perhaps accurate information, one can learn much about the habits of bream shoals in rivers and loughs and make good catches without the use of groundbait. This is because the angler is fishing a restricted area of water or one not so restricted, but he is aware that there is a reasonable probability of bream being there and feeding keenly. Common examples of this are "fast-water" breaming and night fishing in recognised haunts during ideal conditions, canal fishing in bays, and angling in short, deep stretches of rivers between loughs.

There must be many anglers in addition to myself who fish regularly in Ireland and who could name a dozen or so places which would fall under this category of selected waters and who, given the right time and conditions, would reasonably expect to catch bream "off the cuff", as it were. I look upon such places

as the ones to visit for a short period of time, usually during
the evening or at first light. I expect the catch to be small because one cannot prevent indefinitely the natural wanderings
of bream and again, in selected areas of small compass, one
cannot expect a large number of bream to be present, especially
if their average size is of fair proportions.

In other circumstances experience has taught me that much
time will be wasted and catches will be well below par, if
groundbait is not used, and that it is very necessary to curb
the natural desire to move to another place if results are not
forthcoming. If one must move then it should only be because
it is honestly felt that the new spot one has in mind may provide
one with a better opportunity of finding bream, and that the
other place has been given a reasonable trial. The above
example clearly indicates this.

The act of groundbaiting may be done some hours before
starting to fish and is generally termed prebaiting, or just prior
to the act of angling, or indeed subsequently thereto. These
acts are performed, respectively, to persuade bream to congregate pending one's arrival, to entice bream there after one
commences to fish, or to persuade bream to stay after one has
begun to catch fish.

Prebaiting is carried out fairly extensively in Ireland, for
there is little likelihood of someone else enjoying the fruits of
one's labours. A most elementary form of this practice is carried
out by certain anglers who are pursuing another species of fish
and who may administer groundbait to a chosen spot on more
than one occasion before attempting to fish it. One of my hosts
told me that he once had three anglers staying with him for the
primary purpose of enjoying some of the excellent tench fishing
that the area in question had to offer. Their thoughts, however,
eventually turned to bream and it was agreed that two places
on different loughs would be groundbaited and the host and one
of the visitors would fish one of them and the other two anglers
would fish the other chosen spot. Groundbait was used on two
consecutive days and on the evening of the second day the

Competition fishing on the River Erne, Enniskillen, County Fermanagh

respective parties set out. It transpired that bream were active at both places and thirteen fish, the largest 2 lb., were taken from one spot and fourteen fish, the largest $4\frac{1}{4}$ lb., were caught at the other.

Rather sensibly they had groundbaited holes known to harbour bream and had chosen quite a reliable time to fish, and it happened that matters went smoothly for them, but I fancy that few tears would have been shed if results had been negative. This somewhat indifferent approach to bream fishing is most likely to fall down because operations are carried out "during the anglers' pleasure" and not that of the bream. The deposited groundbait could have been devoured at any time after its application and possibly was, either once or twice at one or both places and return visits, although likely by bream shoals, are dependent upon the desires of the fish and not the angler.

The rapidity with which bream can clear a layer of groundbait is well known, I am sure, and for this reason alone the angler who takes prebaiting seriously, ensures that no great period of time elapses before he begins to fish. If he is reasonably sure that no bream are about, he may add further groundbait subsequent to his arrival, for only during clear-water conditions could it be ascertained with any certainty, whether or not the original groundbait had been touched.

The operational bream fisherman can ponder over many matters from natural conditions to the bream's digestion. How long he will stay and how many times he will return, depends on many factors such as results, temperament, ability and the like. I have known cases, as I have previously mentioned, of anglers fishing and baiting the same swim day after day and sometimes their confidence has been amply rewarded. It is a chance anglers are occasionally prepared to take, but over a period of a fortnight, I fancy that the majority of anglers who desire to concentrate their activities at selected places would prefer to fish three or four localities and according to some definite system.

Perhaps the main complaint made by visiting anglers is that

F

of being unable to make a good catch of bream, similar to those they have either read or been told about, and not surprisingly, one of the greatest regrets local angling secretaries have, is that the complaining anglers either cannot or will not make sufficient preparations or try hard enough.

Having admitted elsewhere that some of the largest bream my colleagues and I have taken in Ireland, were caught unexpectedly, without preparation and, indeed, sometimes when angling for other species of fish, I would hasten to add, lest the remarks in this section are considered to be hypocritical, that such events have occurred but rarely. There is no such thing as regular luck in angling, but on the other hand there is much misfortune because that little extra knowledge is missing and in particular I would refer to the missing of bites and also the loss of hooked fish.

I was once discussing the subject of bream fishing with the chairman of an angling club and he mentioned that he had once hooked a large bream which had taken him completely unawares, and in no time it had bored into a nearby weed bed and broken his line. Some little time after our conversation, I happened to find myself fishing with him and his son, and during the course of the day the latter person hooked a large bream no more than five feet from his rod top. Within a few seconds the line broke and during that time I can remember quite vividly the apprehensive look on the chairman's face, the frustrated look on his son's face and the sight of a fully extended rod. On yet another occasion I recall a fellow angler hooking a bream, unbeknown to him, from a swim where a $10\frac{1}{4}$ lb. bream had been taken during the previous year. In a very short time the fish broke free, leaving the angler crestfallen. I could mention several similar stories, all quite authentic in that the fish concerned were definitely large bream, but those I have related give sufficient indication of the inadequacy of the tackle employed or the inability of the angler to rise to the occasion.

On the other hand there are many recorded incidents of anglers finding that bream are nosing, toying, carefully inspecting or, indeed, removing, damaging or even carrying away their baits, but the net result of these activities is as before—namely, no addition to the keep net.

Concerning the loss of big bream, I think the element of surprise and natural impatience have much to do with it, and I have had enough personal experience to suggest that some of the alleged big bream which are lost, are actually fish dressed in different colours.

Such mistakes are natural ones; sometimes the result of an association of ideas which form in the mind because the unsuspecting angler has his thoughts concentrated on bream, and sometimes because the angler is ignorant of the practices of other fish.

It is reasonable to assume that a large number of bream fishermen tend to follow tradition, in that they seek out the deepest water available, being of the opinion that they will have the best chance of finding bream there, and that they are unlikely to be troubled by bottom weed. However, the angler who seeks bream in Ireland will find that he is often confronted by reasonably shallow water (I refer to any depth up to eight feet) when lough fishing, and generally speaking, there is no reason why he should show concern. Underwater carpets of weed are not so heavily or ubiquitously laid, as to absolutely preclude angling at such depths. I have spent many pleasant days fishing waters which were reasonably devoid of aquatic vegetation and of medium depth, and the bait had to be cast but a few yards.

Bream will almost bury their heads in sand, silt or mud, found at the very edge of lough shores and they can sometimes be observed wending their way into the shallows with their tails exposed above the water surface. A carefree approach to the water's edge must result in bream sensing danger, and with a smack of the tail and a contraction of the muscles, departing with all haste. A lordly fish without companions once did precisely this, when I disturbed it while pike fishing on a lough in western Ireland one autumn day.

Certainly, numerous, heavy catches of bream have been taken from the shallower sections of loughs, with or without water of appreciable depth elsewhere and much as bream, located in shallow water, are accustomed to living there, they are neither hardier nor less temperamental than their more favourably situated colleagues. I think it is probable that the bream of the shallow water lough is about the most difficult fish to catch in Ireland.

Concerning baits, the one which undoubtedly causes the most controversy in Ireland is the maggot. It is not especially large and many anglers who have decided to use this bait, automatically go through the motions of carefully "nicking" a bunch of them on say, a size 8 or 10 hook. In one sense the end product looks irresistible; in another, wholly cumbersome and spurious, and it is this latter adjective which I feel is foremost in the minds of the "uneducated" Irish bream when they encounter such lures. The position is understandable when one considers that the bream waters of Ireland have not experienced the "maggot-tipping" operations of a multitude of matchmen.

I never fail to take a generous supply of maggots with me whenever I visit Ireland and occasionally I have been able to obtain them over there, but the number of gallons I have used would probably have only a minor lasting effect, in the aggregate, on a couple of bream shoals in one solitary small lough.

I believe that the main value of the maggot lies in the fact that, in itself it is a "natural" bait, and I believe that it is necessary to take the fullest advantage of this attribute, unless one is in the happy position of being able to fish a swim, which during the season has been frequented by bream that have come to accept the bait without suspicion through regular applications thereof. Such swims, of course, are only likely to be found at well patronised angling centres, and thus, unless this situation exists or unless it is possible to familiarise bream with this bait (and it will take more than a few handfuls of maggots to do so) it may be prudent to fish a single maggot or perhaps two of them on a suitably sized hook, and by that I mean a size 14 and not 20!

That bream may feed with the utmost caution is a fact well known to anglers; bread can be sucked off a hook or dissolved magically and worms can be removed most skilfully. Similarly, a maggot can be drained of its nourishment, and if it is one of a pair, the significance of such an act may go unnoticed in that it may be assumed that it is a case of the fish concerned only managing to grip one of the maggots, whereas in point of fact the fish has deliberately selected one and rejected the other.

This is not an act similar to that performed by a small rudd which attempts to devour unsuccessfully a maggot-laden hook, and leaves one of the maggots in a state of raggedness and probably damages the remainder. It is one of far greater subtlety and I have even known such fastidiousness to be shown by perch.

I recall that I once hooked a bream, just 1 oz. under 7 lb. in weight on a single maggot which was intended for one of a shy shoal of roach I was pursuing in a lake. Needless to say, I was not fishing an Irish water and maggots were well known to the fish there. I had taken one roach when the "intruder" accepted the bait and three more bream, none quite as large as the first, were all taken in the same manner before the morning sun or some other factor caused bites to cease.

I have mentioned this incident more by way of contrast, for it happened at a lake which is visited by many English anglers and who use maggots as bait regularly each season, but it seems to confirm what I have said previously about the bream's definite interest in a bait which is hardly likely to satisfy its appetite and which looks ludicrous when placed alongside that immense "white-walled cavern of a mouth".

I can recall similar incidents happening in Ireland and, conversely, this negative response which is often so apparent when a bunch of maggots is introduced to bream waters, emphasises what I have already implied concerning such a bait. It is necessary to be most careful before making any statement about any point concerning angling, but the use of this type of bait to locate bream is an act one would do well to avoid, whether one is fishing river or lough, so far as normal "laying on" tactics are concerned. Lobworms, brandlings, or redworms will sooner or later attract an individual bream from a passing shoal, and as I have mentioned elsewhere, this is no difficult task, provided one is fishing a bream run and conditions are favourable. On the other hand a bunch of maggots presented similarly will not produce the same degree of response.

When I first commenced to fish for bream in Ireland, I tried various methods and techniques and experimented with baits and found myself performing such elementary acts as the one above, thus coming to the conclusion that the legered maggot, employed as indicated, was the least attractive of the popular baits, and it would seem that through the years bream have not changed their attitude other than as already indicated. The irony of the matter is that if there has been a change at all, it is in connection with the outlook of bream in "popular" waters towards worm bait. As one can imagine, stretches of water visited regularly by anglers using worm baits, must in time become places where the local bream shoals begin to get somewhat wary of them and the angler may have to fish more cautiously than did his predecessors.

When then is the maggot likely to emulate other baits as a means of taking bream? I have had a fair amount of success with this bait when allowing it to drift slowly with the current, and I therefore look upon it as being primarily a lively, mobile, river bait. I have also found that canal bream are quite eager to take it when presented thus. I also recall that when lough fishing I have met with some success when this bait has been able to drift through the action of the wind on a float.

However, concerning still water angling I would restrict its use to the summer months so far as lough bream are concerned, for from my own experience, a lively grub, however presented, seems to have little appeal to lough bream during late autumn and winter.

The remaining popular bait is bread in one form or another

and like the maggot it has not been introduced to Irish waters on a scale grand enough to suggest that it can be used as confidently as a worm bait. One may ask how long a bream takes to familiarise itself with bread and the answer is either two seconds, two days, or perhaps two weeks. This most "unnatural" of baits may have an immediate effect on them, or their interest may be slow in that their approach is one of suspicion, which action is as much as one may expect on waters fished infrequently.

No doubt the freshly cut loaf and paste-filled cloth have graced every fishing platform from Carrickmacross to Portumna at one time or other, and everything from flour paste to breadcrust has been tried at various points along the River Shannon system and on loughs great and small. They and their counterparts are favourite baits of many anglers, who like myself were brought up to show a healthy respect for the by-products of this wholesome commodity.

There is a world of difference between the carefully cut cube, or portion of kneaded paste, or flake ready for the affray, and their ultimate condition after being despatched to some muddy bed below dark waters, or to one of sand or gravel below clear water with healthy green plants in attendance.

Flake is the most delicate of baits. It is quickly affected by water and small particles are soon "lost" and hang in the water before coming to rest down on the bed. Breadcrust is highly absorbent yet needs to be "anchored" to the bed, as they say, unless it is first introduced to the water surface to receive a preliminary baptism. Well kneaded paste is reasonably hardy and with tackle balanced correctly and a smooth cast, it can be despatched to a desired location with safety.

I have observed incidents which suggest that a certain type of bread bait may be preferred by bream to other forms on certain days or at certain locations, but as a generalisation it is usually found that if bream are taking bread, then it does not matter in which form it is presented and there is little to be lost by offering a generous portion of whatever type of bait has been decided upon. I have experienced several interesting encounters with bream when using bread and would say that they can be most artful at removing it from a hook without suspicion, and are undoubtedly more expert at this act than any mouse is at relieving a trap of a piece of cheese.

Flake and crust are two baits bream take much delight in purloining. The former in particular is by its very nature frail, and crust, once it is "drowned", is not held securely by any hook. If an angler finds that bream are "stealing" his bait, then rather obviously a smaller portion should be used and if practicable, a more sensitive form of tackle arrangement.

Somewhat more intriguing are the half-hearted bites of indifferent bream. Much as it is true to say that they are also experienced when bream have been affected by temperature, I think that it is sometimes felt that adverse conditions are to blame for bream biting thus, when in point of fact the fish concerned have patrolled their beat and taken their fill, and because they are digesting what they have eaten, they consider with indifference the bread bait offered to them by the angler who has located them in their resting place.

Obviously, it does not matter what bait is offered in such a situation, and it is disturbing to know that bream are present. The bigger fish enjoy a fairly contented life, with really no other species to vie with in their search for food, and it is they who decide when they will show interest in groundbait and hook baits. If the bream are neither "head downwards" nor completely off their food, it is logical to assume they are lying down below the surface, enjoying the current in the open water, or simply biding their time under surface weed, bushes and the like. They may even be resting on your groundbait wondering what it is doing there!

I think that one answer to the all important problem of persuading them to show interest in your bait, is to present it as attractively as modern tackle will permit. In the faster water one can use a light leger tackle and permit a bait to move about freely by placing the weight at least 2½ feet from the bait. One can also let the bait down the swim periodically as an added incentive.

In the more gentle runs float tackle can be so set that it allows the bait to drag along the bottom, thereby covering the swim and keeping the bait active and hoping that its movement will arouse the curiosity of the fish. In the quiet reaches of a river, one can drop a bait in front of surface weed and hope that bream will be aroused as it sinks slowly either towards or past them. I would also add that whatever comments I have previously made about the use of maggots or forms of bread bait when fishing for "uneducated" bream, in the above cases there is much to be said for "ringing the changes", bearing in mind that one is endeavouring to present a bait right to the nose of bream, as opposed to waiting for them to locate it in their own time and deliberate upon its value as nourishment. I think it worthwhile to remember that away from the popular swims there is this other "natural" aspect to consider when one is set on catching a few "tin plates".

The legendary bubble about lough bream always growing to a greater size than their river colleagues, undoubtedly burst somewhere *en route* across the Irish Sea, for apart from the fact that the rather scant records available tend to refute this, my own experiences leave me in no doubt whatsoever that a generous head of really large bream exists in Irish rivers. Just as emphatically, I would say that whether one angles for them in lough or river, one will find them extremely shy, highly sensitive to physical conditions and worthier of greater respect than some anglers may believe. I choose these words carefully, for success or otherwise depends on these factors.

Mature fish have a wariness which stems from years of experience in the act of self-preservation, and much as large pike may show personal contempt for the proximity of an angler, large rudd, perch and other mature fish in addition to large bream, need no second warning once the angler has shown himself on bank or shore. However, although small pike, perch and rudd will sometimes consider the presence of man with indifference, this is rarely the attitude taken by bream.

It may be felt that feeding bream will sometimes put stomach before security. They can certainly feed ravenously, but the large catches that are recorded are taken by good angling, and not because of the breams' gluttony. They will rest, meditate and peruse, before deciding to devour groundbait, and although I am not convinced that it is always a fatal act to lose a fish, a shoal of bream will not accept indiscretions as readily as certain rudd shoals do.

However, I would like to relate the following experience, and I leave the reader to draw his own conclusions. I was fishing with a friend and an acquaintance one day from a boat moored on the River Shannon. The latter person hooked a large bream and tried to "tank" it in, against a reasonably strong current. He was too excited to be pacified and the fish freed itself when quite near to the craft. Undaunted, he cast again and eventually hooked a second fish, and as he once more refused to act with patience, this fish was also lost, again when some little distance from the boat. A third cast produced a third fish and as a result of our rather strong words, he followed our instructions and eventually brought the fish alongside the boat. I remember my colleague gazing into the water and saying, "It's a bream; a 'thumping' great bream!" At the very last moment, the novice put too much pressure on the line and the fish broke loose.

One might consider that the trio of freed bream would be more than sufficient to alarm the shoal, but shortly afterwards I hooked one of them, and this was the last incident of note. It may be assumed that the shoal was not a large one, owing to the great size of the fish, and it will be noted that none of the fish was lost near to where the shoal was positioned.

Most Irish bream are caught between May and September, and perhaps the best evening and night fishing is to be had during July and August, when the temperature is more inclined to be suited to their feeding habits. Earlier or later in the year the temperature can fall quite suddenly and curtail the enjoyment of the evening. June is probably the best of the remaining months because of the long evenings. On the River Shannon it is no rare sight for one to observe anglers at this time of the year making for their swims a couple of hours before sunset, and staying there for several hours with bream coming to net at regular intervals.

This is also the position with lough fishing and I could not relate the times I have left the shores of a lough, long after the last of the sun's rays had disappeared. However, there have also been times when it has been difficult to believe that it was midsummer, and I have left my swim prematurely, fishless and frozen, but with the certain knowledge that bream were thereabouts. The oft fickle June temperature has been the reason, and the same position arises once August has passed by.

During late September one can expect the daylight hours to continue until about 8.15 p.m. in the west, and 8 p.m. along the River Shannon system. The last hour before and the first hour following darkness often provide the apex of the day's fishing, although fish can be caught much later than this. In fact, two of the finest bream I ever saw taken from the River Shannon were caught at about 11 p.m. towards the end of September. However, all too frequently the "nip in the air" causes one to retire before this hour, and perhaps seek the more convivial atmosphere of a local tavern. September morns are often mild and calm, though by mid-morning, the tranquil scene may well have changed and especially on exposed waters. Good catches of bream and tench for that matter, have been taken during the first hours of light, and I know of certain anglers who make a point of fishing the morning and evening "shifts" and of sleeping during the intervening period!

It is no difficult task to take a bream or two from a suitable swim without any preparation during the daytime. The catch may be larger, but such are the general habits of bream, that it is generally necessary to use groundbait to persuade others to stay and, one hopes feed. It is no fallacy, however, that one can encounter very large shoals of bream feeding at this time.

Chapter Seven

ANGLING FOR RUDD

OF THE VARIOUS SPECIES of coarse fish found in Ireland, my angling friends and I, with one exception, have taken more large rudd than any other. One colleague has enjoyed his greatest success when pike fishing, but he is an exceptional angler in this respect and he has inferred that he has "a couple of tricks up his sleeve" when it comes to pursuing Esox, and they have never been divulged. He is also an intrepid angler, as evidenced by the fact that on two occasions I have had to retrieve him from the depths of shivering bogs!

I have experienced phenomenal rudd fishing in Ireland, and such occasions have arisen when a shoal has been content to remain at a certain spot over a considerable period of time. Four of us once found one of these shoals on a day in late September, and between 5 p.m. and dusk we caught about 300 rudd. The shoal covered an area of some thirty yards by ten yards and remained before us until the coolness of the twilight hour caused the fish to stop biting.

The rudd averaged $1\frac{1}{4}$ lb. in weight and accepted maggots, worms and paste, and were taken at all depths down to about two feet from the bed, the actual depth being seven feet. As I have mentioned elsewhere, I find it a wise move to fish in and around a rudd shoal at varying depths in the hopes of taking an exceptional fish, but in this case they weighed between 12 oz. and $1\frac{1}{2}$ lb., with the exception of a few small rudd, which I imagine were the permanent inhabitants of the neighbouring reeds.

On another occasion two of us were trolling for pike along a back-cut of the River Shannon, when I saw a shoal of rudd "making merry" above us on the starboard side of our boat. We tethered the boat above the shoal and were soon ready to angle for them. It was a reasonably bright day with a slight breeze rippling the water, and in time the rudd shoal moved along the reed bed and eventually began to swim around and under our boat without concern. We could have filled the boat with these obliging fish which averaged ¾ lb. in weight, but our relationship became too intimate, as it were, and eventually we went on our way. We had had many hours good rudd fishing during the previous days and as the shoal members seemed to be of a uniform weight, we were content to move on.

Rudd fishing can be like this. These fish can spoil one and cause one to be fastidious, but in the depths of winter when far away from them, there is a tendency to recall how pleasant encounters with them have really been, even if they were not quite "rod benders". These latter fish (I would call any rudd over 1½ lb. in weight a "rod bender") are, like most adult fish, rather unpredictable. A shoal of large rudd can be kept at close quarters for some time, but on other occasions they will adamantly keep out of range or even play hide and seek with you and an appreciable amount of water can be covered as they are pursued from one spot to another. There is also the individual fish which has left its shoal to venture as a single unit on some special mission. One such fish came the way of a colleague and the circumstances which led up to its capture are, I think, interesting enough to record.

We had been concentrating on a shoal of moderately sized rudd and as darkness approached it moved off, and shortly afterwards I began to dismantle my tackle. As I was doing this, I saw a fish to my right, nosing the surface and exposing its dorsal fin, and this it repeated, slowly and deliberately close to the bank at regular intervals. My colleague still had his equipment intact and I informed him of this. He passed quietly behind me in pursuit of the fish and like a lough fly fisherman, who has been observing the movements of a trout, he delicately cast his bait just in front of the fish. It was taken

and after an interesting battle in the half-light, I netted the
fish and it was found to weigh 2 lb. 3 oz. It was not an exceptional fish, but nevertheless a specimen, and the nocturnal act of
searching for insects on the surface led to its downfall, although
it had actually accepted maggot just below the surface.

I recall that a couple of years later, I took a rudd 1 oz.
heavier, when fishing about eighteen inches below the surface
at a spot not far downstream from where the other rudd was
taken. It was a warm August afternoon and as I had lost the
shoal of rudd I had located, I was hopefully searching the water
thereabouts. There is surely nothing more splendid in Irish
coarse fishing than the sight of a 2 lb. rudd with its golden body
reflecting the sunlight, and its red fins adding that extra touch
of colour.

The methods of setting up float tackle for rudd fishing vary
somewhat, but broadly speaking they fall into two categories.
There is the light form of tackle which may consist of a minute
quill float with one small shot in attendance, or perhaps a larger
quill float used without shot, which allows one's bait to sink
gently and the float to lie flat or in a half-cocked position.
There are also certain anglers who use a section of reed in
place of a float, because of its lightness and naturalness.

On the other side we have what may be described as "shot-
bearers". These are floats of varying length and construction,
but all capable of carrying a fair minimum weight. We are
generally obliged to think in terms of a float when rudd fishing
because of their natural habit of feeding or swimming near or
at the water surface, although they will accept flies, both
natural and artificial, chrysalis, and also floating cubes of bread
which they love to nose and nibble and for whose acquisition
they will often strongly vie with each other.

When it comes to float fishing for large rudd, one has to
consider the distance a bait may have to be cast in relation to
prevailing weather conditions. Because of this, it is frequently
necessary to employ a float capable of being cast into a breeze
on say, 4 lb. b.s. line. However, lighter tackle may normally be

used on, say, calm evenings when the angler, fishing perhaps
waters of small acreage, can readily come across rudd shoals
and when as previously indicated, they may remain within
easy reach for long periods and provide sport unceasingly.

The shoals of the larger specimens of rudd which inhabit such
waters are not too difficult to locate because like all rudd, they
cannot resist jumping, or at least nosing the surface according to
their fancy from time to time and during most kinds of weather,
although when winds are boisterous, activity is less pronounced.
Nevertheless I emphasise this point which has previously been
referred to, because rudd can be taken during inclement
weather.

Once during mid-September I was fishing for bream on one
of the River Shannon's backwaters, and as the westerly wind
was sweeping in from the Atlantic, I had positioned myself on
the lee side in the shelter of quite a high bank, the discovery of
which I might add, can be quite an achievement on the River
Shannon system. None of the excellent bream thereabouts had
troubled to investigate my groundbait, but I was being entertained by the ever obliging perch at fairly regular intervals.

Then, on the far side, there was the almost inaudible sound
of a splash and the fleeting glimmer of a fish just in front of
some lily pads, which were being tossed like pancakes in the
gale. Taking in the line I changed my float to one which would
not be lost in or intimidated by the rough water, and setting it
three feet from the hook and baiting up with maggot, I cast
across the backwater and allowed the hook to fall short of the
lilies.

I let the float drift in a little and it was gone. The rudd which
took the bait was one of five or six which eventually finished up
in the keep-net. In this instance the shoal was near to cover, but
this is not always the case during adverse conditions. Towards
the end of September 1952, I located a shoal of rudd in the
mouth of a cut on the River Shannon. A strong north-westerly
wind sprang up and the rudd disappeared. On the assumption
that they had moved to less agitated water along the lee shore

of the main river, I commenced to look for them there and eventually settled down in a sheltered swim protected on either side by a bed of reeds, each growing out into the river.

Presently a rudd jumped, but not immediately before me or along the reed fringe for that matter. The fish had surfaced twenty yards from the bank just to my right at a spot where the wind was having a telling effect on the water and I recall taking four rudd from this offshore position.

Certainly excellent catches of rudd are made during the summer months, when rivers are low and easy paced and loughs are generally calm and not full of fresh water, but this "fair weather fish" description is misleading. Many years ago I remember being introduced to a small lake during mid-February, and using paste as bait and fishing between decayed bulrushes, a fair number of rudd weighing up to 1½ lb. were caught.

Another point I must mention regarding the rudd, concerns the habits of the larger specimens of this fish, when they form part of a shoal. I have located many shoals of rudd during my angling career, but on two occasions I have had the good fortune to encounter really large shoals. The first time this happened was in October 1952, and the shoal was not only spread out across the river in question, but vanished into the watery distance downstream. The main observation was that several of the larger fish were situated in the van, or at either side of the shoal. The fish were stationary save for the necessary movement of fin, or desire on the part of some to elevate or lower themselves in the water, and although, as previously mentioned, the whole of the shoal could not be seen, the superficial area it covered was at the very least one hundred and fifty square yards.

In August 1955 I saw the second shoal while bank fishing on the River Suck. The shoal, moving quietly downstream, took an appreciable time to pass, for there was score upon score of them, red-finned, and deep bellied. As before, the bigger fish had comprised the front rank of the shoal, and they were also

Into a reach on the Fairy Water Omagh

positioned freely along the side nearer to me. It is probably reasonable to assume that this was also the position on the far flank of the shoal. I feel that these two incidents indicate that the adult rudd, far from being a timid fish when among its own kind, is not only prepared to tolerate their company, but also to act as leader and sentinel. It cannot physically defend the shoal, although I have often had to admire them for personally evading the clutches of pike, as the savage lacerations on their sides and back have proved, but they seem to want to guide and influence the smaller rudd, and whatever the extent of their activities be in this respect, I am obliged to say that there is more to the general character of large rudd than the acute awareness of danger and the profound shyness they undoubtedly possess.

While dealing with the subject of rudd shoals, I feel I ought to differentiate between the act of "fishing the shoal" and that of "investigating the shoal". In the former case one knows where the shoal is and the most advantageous depth at which to fish, and one's efforts are concentrated on the area of water in which the shoal is situated. In the latter case one is looking for the larger rudd. They may not exist, they may be within the main body of the shoal; they may be down below in the centre, or at the rear of the shoal, or on the flanks.

Perhaps the great majority of anglers would be content to fish among the shoal. It takes courage to act otherwise, especially when the fish are of excellent weight. However, I feel that it is not an unreasonable act to compromise and occasionally "investigate the shoal". One can compromise in another way, namely by changing to a number 6 hook and allowing a substantial portion of paste or other bait to pass through the shoal.

The reference to hooks reminds me of the time I was asked to obtain a few small rudd-bream hybrids for examination purposes. Prior to my departure I had entered into a friendly argument with a Yorkshire match-angler on the subject of small hooks. Knowing of my impending expedition, he pro-

G

duced a few of his self-tied number 20 hooks, stating they would
be ideal for taking the fish I would be pursuing, and as an
afterthought he remarked. "They'll hold anything you get.
Grand hooks are them!"

My angling colleague and I went on our way and eventually
we came to a spot which I knew was frequented often by
hybrids and using the number 20 hooks, we soon caught half a
dozen on a single maggot bait. No sooner had they been stored
away, when far across the river, we heard "a splashing in the
reeds."

We packed up our tackle, climbed into the boat we had at
our disposal, and I rowed across the river, moving the craft as
quietly as possible during the latter part of the journey, and
guided the bow into the reeds several yards upstream.

I decided to change the number 20 hook for a number 10,
especially as the active rudd were of excellent size, but my
colleague, partly through impatience and partly through
loyalty to our Yorkshire friend, immediately baited up, cast
and hooked a fish, all in a matter of seconds. It was carefully
played and landed and as the keep-net was placed over the
side of the boat I was ready to present my bait and this I did.
Another fish took without hesitation and was subsequently
landed. As I was placing this fish in the keep-net my colleague
hooked "something big", as they say.

In view of the proximity of the reed bed and the fact that
there was a fair current, not to mention the size of the hook,
the fish was played with the utmost care. On several occasions
it allowed itself to be brought near the boat and I had laid
down my rod and had the landing net before me, but each
time the fish returned. From the glimpses I had of it, I was
beginning to form the opinion that it was near to 3 lb. in weight.
At last it showed signs of tiring and once more line was taken
in and the fish slowly approached the boat. The landing net
was in the water and when the fish was but two feet away from
it, the hook pulled loose from the skin of the fish's mouth and
it drifted away in the current. We were both disappointed but

not surprised and my colleague, needless to say, immediately changed his hook.

The shoal had moved some distance out into the river but we were still within casting range, and there they remained while we caught thirty-one of them. Three of them were under 1 lb. in weight and the largest of the remaining fish weighed 1 lb. 10 oz. In view of this, it may be argued that my assessment of the weight of the lost fish was inaccurate, or that it was one isolated, large fish, or that any other large rudd which may have been present, had become wary.

It is difficult to determine the size of fish when in the water, because of distortion, colourisation and their shape. This applies particularly to deep bellied fish in which general category rudd may be deemed to fall, but I shall remember the golden sides of that fish, gleaming beneath the surface for many a year yet; as well, in fact, as the remarks directed at our Yorkshire friend upon our return!

Another aspect of rudd fishing I feel I ought to make some reference to, is what may be described as "non-visual" angling. Once rudd have been caught at a certain place, there is a reasonable chance of taking them again from there at a later time, although there may not be the slightest indication they are still inhabiting the stretch of water concerned when a subsequent visit is made. That extreme weather or water conditions may then exist is always a possibility in Ireland, and I am thinking of flood conditions as much as anything as I write, because the presence of a strong current at a spot where it is ordinarily less pronounced, will cause rudd there to seek calmer situations and much fresh water in a lough will again tend to cause a temporary migration. It is then that the angler finds himself taking rudd from the meadow side of the reeds and from drains that are normally quite shallow, but without a steady flow of water, and there rudd congregate away from the racing river.

There is one section of the River Shannon that I have known during the whole of my angling "life" in Ireland and over a

distance of a quarter of a mile, I have come to look upon five
places as being the natural lairs of rudd. There are spots too,
where I have never seen a rudd show itself, nor have I ever
taken one when I have angled there.

The main conclusion one comes to, is that the faster water
to which I have previously referred and the lower regions of
deep water are the least likely places in which to find rudd.
In fact only once have I seen what I thought to be large rudd
in a really strong current on a river of appreciable width.
There were half a dozen or so breaking the water surface at
frequent intervals while they stayed there, but notwithstanding
their general appearance, they may well have been rudd-
bream hybrids in view of their size.

I can recall but a handful of occasions when I have taken
rudd from the depths and I suspect that they were attracted
there by groundbait, having become interested in some of the
slowly sinking particles, or because of pronounced temperature
change. One interesting point about such captures has been the
generous size of the fish concerned, but they have happened
far too infrequently for the suggestion to be made that the rudd
angler would generally benefit from acting thus. He is more
likely to find that bream are showing an interest in his sinking
bait.

Reverting to the subject of fast water, I have found that
much as the main channel of the river with its clear bed of
sand, gravel or clay holds little interest for rudd, adjoining
waters, especially those of less pronounced depth, where silt
has accumulated, where weed growth is evident and where the
flow of the river is not so determined, are well worth trying.
They can be found just past the bend of a river or below a
bridge or a promontory that determines the course of the main
current. Even if the area past the bend of a river is not as
predescribed, it may still follow that a point just beyond the
inner bend harbours rudd, as will a place farther downstream
on the opposite side of the river, where the current abates.

I think it is far more important to consider the natural

movements of rivers than the position of their weed growth, much as the latter can be governed by the former, because rudd are far less willing to taste the delights of the shimmering stream than certain other species.

Certain friends and I have experienced memorable days fishing for rudd on rivers where the current was steady and the act of long trotting could be employed to advantage. Sometimes rudd shoals have been so large and obliging that it has been possible to fish over long periods without having to wait any noticeable period of time for a bite. The fish have accepted baits so surely that a steady tightening of the line was all that was necessary to secure the hook. Once this has been achieved, I have found that the most sensible procedure to adopt is to steer or permit them to move away from the spot where they have been hooked and then, and only then, exert pressure on the fish, otherwise they may perform all kinds of contortions about the water surface, or simply "stand on their tails", thereby putting great strain on one's tackle, and this can result in the hook becoming dislodged.

Having fished for rudd in moving water on so many occasions through the years, I have been tempted into pursuing the less orthodox acts of "laying on" or letting the bait drag along the river bed in the hopes of increasing my knowledge of them.

The tendency is to think of bottom fishing for rudd during late autumn and winter when, if they are feeding, they are most likely to be doing so in the deeper sections of rivers near to the bed, unless the weather is unusually mild. I can also recall occasions during flooding, when rudd have been taken on the bottom right under the bank.

As with bream, rudd will frequent shallow water and during the summer months in particular, certain of my angling friends and I have taken good fish during the last hour or so of daylight when fishing a sizeable bait of worm or paste on or near the bed. To a lesser degree these shallow-water tactics can produce results during the early hours of the morning, but this time of the day finds bream and tench more active.

My final reference is to still-water angling, which concerns primarily the waters of loughs; but it is convenient to include such frequently quoted places as bays, backwaters, recesses and the like situated along river courses.

Bearing in mind that the main subject under discussion is "non-visual" angling for rudd, I would say, rather obviously, that it is more difficult to locate rudd in a lough of large proportions than one of small acreage, or those stretches of a river least influenced by current. The natural wanderings of fish in still water can hinder one, and in these modern times when anglers are both requested and expected to "think and debate before sinking the bait", some knowledge of any large water is desirable before one angles for rudd there. Even if such fish have actually betrayed their presence, one's chances of success may be short lived.

For example, a friend and I had moored our boat at a respectable distance from a spot where a line of rushes curved in towards the shore of a lough we found ourselves fishing towards the end of summer in 1958. It was warm and calm and the waters of the lough were restful and unruffled for as far as the eye could see. There had not been the trace of the tiniest dimple on the water surface from the time we had set out, which explains why we happened to find ourselves searching the water of this baylet.

An hour or so passed by without incident and then, far away on the opposite shore, a combination of momentary glitter and sound informed us that rudd were there. We decided to investigate and in due course we approached the spot in question. There is little doubt that one rudd had said to the others, "Watch out, here's two keen types", and another had said, "Give them a half minute of hope and then we'll scarper", and that is precisely what happened, notwithstanding that the last stage of our journey was made with great caution. They never reappeared either at that spot or in the vicinity thereof, although we spent some time fishing there.

Angling for rudd on the larger size of lough can be a frustrat-

ing business, but usually there is no limit to the size of fish
which can be caught from such waters. Conversely, loughs of
much smaller acreage may teem with rudd but few, if any,
sizeable fish may be present because the number of fish may be
out of all proportion to the amount of food available. However,
it is an undeniable fact that some of the smaller loughs contain
rudd of most excellent size.

Concerning those sections of rivers which fall under the
heading of "still waters", there is much to be said for concentrating on a place where rudd are also likely to be found in
the main river. I feel that rudd prefer to wander within their
own immediate environment, and whereas there are exceptions
to this, as for example, when a river is low and fish seek the
current, it is probable that one will be more successful fishing
thus, and not by selecting a swim which is in itself attractive
but whose adjoining waters would not be favoured by rudd.

River rudd are "born of the current" and enjoy it to a fair
degree. They utilise back-waters and bays and similar places
as a type of retreat, where they either spend time idly or obtain
supplies of natural food from and about plant life. Much as
shoals of young rudd may regularly be found there, they are
by no means the permanent quarters of the larger fish, but they
are interesting, alternative places to those centred about the
steady stream and quieter waters.

Anglers who specialise in still-water rudd fishing carry out
their activities in several different ways. There is that rather
rare problem in angling to solve of how to take a species of
fish which, when it is not disclosing its presence, may not be
the least bit interested in a layer of groundbait spread out over
the river or lough bed. To some anglers the idea of a bait not
resting snugly on that groundbait may be ludicrous; to others,
the suggestion that a bait should be allowed to hang a foot or so
beneath the surface may seem a ridiculous one, and to other
parties, the idea of repeatedly casting a bait into a confined
area of water may be a "disturbing" one.

How then does one go about seeking the unseen rudd which

is allegedly lurking between the surface and the bed? I think the answer can be found by studying the most prominent characteristics of the rudd, which are curiosity and movement, for of all the species of freshwater fish that swim in our waters and whose average weight is over an ounce or two, I would say that only the dace vies with the rudd in this respect. I therefore follow a plan in keeping with these characteristics.

Having decided upon the water I intend to fish, I begin by casting as far as it is convenient for me to do so along the fringe of rushes or surface weed with the bait some eighteen inches from the float. If there is no response after a minute or so. I draw in line and if results are still negative, repeat this operation until the float is about six yards away. I then make a further long-range cast, only this time the float has been placed farther up the line at a point which will permit the bait to hang about two feet from the bed. If there is no response, I recommence the act of withdrawal until I have investigated the upper and lower regions of the swim.

There has been no question of using groundbait as yet, for I have been endeavouring to locate rudd with the minimum of disturbance and I can recall a number of occasions when the first fish or two taken, have been the largest that have come to net. If the initial exploration of the swim has produced no fish, I try to arouse the curiosity of the rudd which I hope are within the area. They may well be under the surface weed or in adjoining rushes or perhaps somewhere in the more open water, but I prefer to concentrate on the water nearest the marginal vegetation. There are several ways of endeavouring to persuade rudd to leave cover and perhaps the most common one is that of throwing pieces of bread on the water surface.

As a rule I prefer to employ such tactics when I can see or hear rudd going about their business in inaccessible places and wish to entice them to open water, or when they appear out of casting range and I wish to entice them to come nearer. There is no reason why we should not cast "our bread upon the waters", when we are unsure if rudd are present, but if they are not breaking surface, it is far more important to agitate them into action at the depth where they are situated. Because of this, the use of a "cloud" groundbait is called for. As an alternative, or in addition, a small number of maggots or a few pellets of paste can be introduced about the float top.

These, then, are the methods whereby certain of my colleagues and I search for still-water rudd. Hitherto, I have not hidden the fact that rudd can be attracted to more wholesome forms of groundbait resting on the bed and at quite appreciable depths, and that sometimes they have been caught without any form of inducement whatsoever, whether in river or lough, but ordinarily I would prefer to move to a new haunt if I had been unsuccessful.

I remember once fishing one of the main loughs of central Ireland with a friend, and the day in question was warm and reasonably calm with the sun partially concealed by high clouds. It was, as far as one could predict, a suitable day for rudd fishing, but they were not in mischievous mood. As we were rowing past a bed of reedmace, a face, bronzed and weather-beaten, appeared above it and its owner told us that "there had been a divil of a rumpus in the small bay beyond not ten minutes ago, and it must have been the roach". Thanking him for the information, we quietly approached the bay around which our informant had walked some little time before. Eventually, we found ourselves peering into the bay, encircled by reeds and with lily pads here and there, but there was not one visible sign of rudd. Undaunted, the stern of the boat was quietly tucked away into the reeds on one side of the bay's entrance, and in due course my colleague was casting to the near side of the bay and I directed my bait to the immediate interior of the bay on the far side. We both hooked fish simultaneously and we continued to catch rudd for a considerable period of time, until, as so often happens when rudd fishing, all went quiet and then not a fish was to be found anywhere.

I have fished that bay on several occasions since. Sometimes rudd have been present, but the unsuspecting angler might have thought otherwise, and sometimes the movements around the lily pads and the rushes, and splashes about the open section of the bay, informed me all too obviously of their presence. I have known rudd to take, with the boat bouncing on the wind-agitated waters of the lough, and there have been times when rudd were wholly absent.

Rudd fishing on the bigger loughs can be a fascinating occupation and it is a far cry from the act of searching for them on one of the many loughs of small acreage in Ireland that contain a good head of these fish, and perhaps it is fitting to conclude this section on the rudd by way of a reminder that this fish, so often referred to as the natural substitute for the roach, is quite a versatile and nomadic species, and from the point of view of habit alone, bears no more resemblance to the roach than Irish bacon does to Yorkshire pudding!

Chapter Eight

ANGLING FOR OTHER FISH

THE REMAINING non-game fish in Ireland, of interest to anglers are carp, gudgeon, eels, roach, tench and dace. They are all localised fish except for eels, and anglers who wish to fish for them should make careful enquiries before deciding where to stay. An experienced angler once told me that some of the gudgeon he had found in the River Blackwater (Munster), were amongst the largest he had ever seen. They also inhabit the River Barrow—where there is a run of thwaite shad during May and June, incidentally.

Interest in tench fishing has grown tremendously in recent years and I am, therefore, prompted to devote more time to this very sporting fish. The first tench I ever saw in Ireland were in a glass case in the Natural History Museum, Dublin, and I can assure any angler that a visit to this establishment will not cause disappointment.

These tench were taken from Lough Derg, which forms part of the Shannon River system, along whose course new tench grounds are regularly being discovered. There are many loughs to which tench have been introduced during the past seven or eight years and already these transplanted fish have caused quite a few hearts to palpitate. In more recent years I have heard rumours about "monster tench" being seen here and there and of broken float tackle sailing away, but earlier reports are rare. However, an Irish angler once told me that during the war years, a friend and he were fishing one of the minor Shannon tributaries and the former gentleman caught a tench. The two of them decided that it was an "odd" species of trout, and being a little dubious about its food value, promptly threw it back.

The angler who regularly fishes one of the better known English tench waters would find it difficult to look upon this species as a "newly-found" fish, still partly shrouded in mystery, but that is still the position to a fair degree in Ireland. Its tench fishing has a most interesting future and angling enthusiasts and officials are not being presumptuous when they talk of new record fish awaiting capture, perhaps of a size one only dreams about. Time will tell, but already fish weighing 4 lb. and 5 lb. are regularly caught and six-pounders find their way to the net. In July 1963 the then record 7 lb. tench taken from Clooncorick Lake, near Carrigallen in Co. Leitrim, was surpassed by one of 7 lb. 6 oz., from Garnafailagh near to Athlone. Shortly afterwards there was a report in the Irish press of a 7 lb. 8 oz. tench being taken from a Co. Monaghan lake; and thus the tempo quickens and the arrival of the first 8 lb. tench is awaited, while the stock fish grow plumper and the undisturbed tench continue to root near the lilies and rushes in their thousands, harbouring among their ranks many fish of commendable weight and some whose size one would only dare mention in whispers. The present record tench weighed 7 lb. 12 oz.

I think it fair to say that the Irish tench is not too difficult to find, provided one takes the precaution of fishing the type of water it favours. Such an obviously trite remark may be considered to be superfluous, but I do know that certain anglers tend to criticise a river or lough if the standard of angling there is disappointing, regardless of their knowledge of the water in question. I also think it important to emphasise that tench tend to be more susceptible to extremes of temperature than bream, and far more than rudd and perch.

On cold, gloomy morns I have inspected my watch when situated before a tench swim and told myself that I should not have stirred from my bed, and with the approach of nightfall on cool evenings after sunless days, I appreciate that I have continued to fish for tench more in hope than with genuine expectancy.

However, Irish tench are quite generous in their dealings

with anglers concerning both conditions of weather, other than as aforesaid, and of baits. The presence of strong winds and dark skies is not everyone's idea of suitable weather conditions for tench, yet it is a fact that many fish are caught during such uncompromising weather and it is, therefore, true to say that they are not specifically "fair weather" fish. When the wind is bringing waves to the shore and unsettling water lilies and reeds, tench tend to move away into deeper water where they will feed if they so wish.

In the more sheltered sections of loughs, an off-shore wind, together with an overcast sky may well be responsible for producing conditions suited to them during the daylight hours. Prolonged gales with frequent, heavy showers produce conditions rarely tolerated by them, however. One can only hope that there is a lull in the weather during the evening before the temperature falls too low, when they may be persuaded to co-operate, if but for a short period. One interesting point about this aspect of tench fishing is that the bait, as often as not lying in no great depth of water close to the weed fringe, is sometimes accepted by young bream as the evening draws on. It is as if they are trying to tell one that the tench have moved off for the night and it is now their turn to commandeer the swim.

Certain colleagues and I have also experienced this when angling for tench during the early hours of the morning. One has no desire to prognosticate, but one ultimately finds that the small "silvers" are the only fish interested in the bait, and their presence is thus deemed to be an unfortunate omen.

Much as the above is the less cheerful side to Irish tench fishing, I have given it preference over the type of angling conditions one generally associates with tench fishing because, quite apart from emphasising as I have elsewhere, that the angler who fishes in Ireland must be prepared to adapt himself to the peculiarities of the country's weather, I feel it should be clearly understood that good tench fishing can be had with a little perseverance during unsettled weather. It is most noticeable that some of Ireland's largest recorded tench have come to net then, and this rather proves the point in question.

During summer mornings and also evenings when one watches the sun setting over the Cavan, Leitrim or Sligo hills, one cannot fail to be a little tense as a careful approach is made to the water's edge. One hopes to espy the familiar bubbles reaching the surface, or even the end of a broad tail protruding above the water surface. Perhaps there are movements among the reeds and lilies or something enlivening but less desirable is observed, such as a small tench leaving the water in terror as it is pursued by a pike. The most impressive sight is that of the bow waves set up by big tench as they cruise just below the surface. They can be seen quite easily, perhaps forty or fifty yards away, and during the daylight tench freely enjoy gliding about thus in open water. As night falls they sometimes swim close to the bank and anyone experiencing this should carefully cast out a fair portion of crust. It will float easily enough even in a breeze and it is an exciting method of taking tench. About twenty years ago I used to fish a small reservoir whose tench had become so domesticated, that they used to come and "collect" pieces of bread thrown on the surface very near to the side. It was considered almost unethical to catch them, but one finds that large tench are prepared to act in this way in Ireland and I do not think that one should worry too much about ethics!

One small word of caution though. An angling acquaintance of mine was fond of this method of angling, and so careful was he in his ways, that wherever possible he hid himself and his rod behind a tall bed of rushes and relied upon a run being indicated on his line. On one such occasion line was drawn off the reel and the rapidity with which it passed through the rings left him so spellbound that it was seconds before he had the sense to strike, and when he did he promptly found himself fast in a somewhat irate swan!

This, rather aptly, brings me to the subject of tackle and particularly to the question of line strength. As I have suggested before, a line with a breaking strain of 4 lb. is sufficiently strong to deal with the average run of Irish fish other than pike, and if one is fortunate enough to locate tench in open water then there is justification for using a line of this or of even lighter breaking strain.

In other circumstances there should be no hesitation in deciding to employ stronger tackle. Irish tench fight, bore, accelerate and even sulk with a determination that sooner or later leaves one in no doubt as to their qualities as sporting fish, and I have met several anglers who have discovered this later, rather than sooner, to their cost. As an example, a group of anglers once fished a well-known tench lough during most unfavourable conditions, but over a period of a few days, nine tench were hooked though only five of them came to net, and three of them were taken from places on the lough where there were few snags to contend with.

None of the anglers used a line exceeding 5 lb. breaking strain, but a "breakage" percentage of forty-four seems to indicate that they were victims of their own vanity, especially as they knew that tench weighing at least 7 lb. were present in the lough, and that some of the selected swims with their profuse weed growth invited disaster.

As a final precautionary note, let me tell you about the time I was stalking a shoal of large rudd I had seen jumping in the corner of a heavily weeded bay. The only way one could reach their estimated location was by casting between a narrow channel of short, tubular reeds, to the right of which was situated a further line of rushes and to the left there was a large clump of lily pads. The day was dull and breezy and as the bay was quite shallow, I decided to fish on the bottom. First of all I tried crust and subsequently changed to maggot, but no bites came. However, shortly after changing to a black-headed worm, I hooked a fish and initially there was what I can only describe as an "explosion" down below. The fish, scorning the reeds sped out into the lough and suddenly stopped, but within a second it raced back towards the channel which it entered. It rose almost

to the surface and then turned sharply to its right, but before
it reached the lily pads, it had freed itself as it charged through
the short reeds.

I had a glimpse of the fish shortly after hooking it. It was a
fairly large tench but there was no possibility of control-
ling its actions. My line of 4 lb. breaking strain never stood a
chance, once it made for the weed bed. I would like to think that
every angler who specialised in tench fishing in Ireland would
err on the side of safety, so to speak, because even from what
facts are available, there seem to be far too many good fish lost
through tackle breakage.

A fellow visitor once caught a tench weighing exactly 6 lb.
and was then broken by a much larger fish. A week later I was
fishing near to the spot in question, and after a rainstorm and
with the thunder rolling round the local hills, the largest tench
I am ever likely to see leapt out of the water and the ensuing
crash could not have been bettered by a builder jettisoning a
load of bricks into the lough. Such a fish was never meant to
be caught on 3 or 4 lb. line and it can be guaranteed that if
there is a single lily pad or reed within striking distance, any
adult tench will endeavour to arrange to accommodate one's
hook therein, with a facility that will leave one aghast, but it
is to be hoped, rather more sagacious when one comes to repair
one's tackle.

I have found that Irish tench are not over-fussy about the
type of bait presented, and even in underfished waters they seem
to attune themselves far more quickly to "new" baits than do
bream. Much as the reliable lobworm and black-headed worm
are perhaps the most popular baits, maggot and bread have
certainly taken their toll.

No doubt their less staid approach to the act of feeding (as
opposed to bream) has much to do with it, bearing in mind their
love of shallow water and that side to their character which
prompts them to move in mid-water and even about the surface
on occasion, and their free acceptance of animal life on and
about water plants, and, of course, vegetable matter itself.

A nice pike from the River Finn, County Monaghan

One problem likely to confront the angler is that which may arise in the presentation of his bait, for he has to ensure that it is detectable to fish in water where the bed is of liquid mud or covered in a carpet of weed. Several excellent tench waters I have fished in Ireland have called for the greatest care in this respect, and short of using radar equipment on the bed, the angler should spare no pains in satisfying himself that his bait is available for inspection by tench. I have already mentioned this point in connection with bream fishing and my comments apply equally here. Fortunately, many lough tench are tucked away in the shallow bays near to the shore and it is often possible to angle for them using a minimum of tackle. If leger tackle is to be used, ensure that it is of the link variety.

The problems presented by a difficult swim can be mitigated by the use of what is generally termed "light tackle". The expression does not embrace lines of a low breaking strain unless, as previously stated, if can be said that the capture of tench on such lines is within one's capabilities.

As may be expected, June and July are the popular months for tench fishing in Ireland, although nowadays there seems to be a marked interest shown in tench during late May. Many fish caught at this time of the year are either in the process of spawning, or have just completed one or more stages of their spawning activities. I have caught tench in late September and can vouch for both their fighting qualities and their willingness to accommodate the angler, particularly on mild September mornings. I also recall that a young angler acquaintance of mine insisted on using his frail-tipped match rod after being directed to a known tench location on the River Shannon. It was not very long before he had to change to another rod!

The Irish tench season continues until the autumnal winds gather force and proceed to play havoc with lough water temperatures, and if the rivers are not prematurely full of flood water when autumn arrives, I for one, would be "on the lookout" for these brassy, red-eyed, pensive looking fish, whose rapidly built reputation and unquestioned virility demand that

H

more than scant reference be made to them when one is discussing Irish coarse fishing.

To conclude this chapter I wish to refer briefly to carp. I have
never fished for them in Ireland because of their general lack of
distribution, but from time to time I have heard of them being
located by unsuspecting anglers, and although I cannot guarantee the accuracy of such reports, some of them at least have been
made by anglers who would profess to know a carp when they
see one. A Birmingham angler I once had the pleasure of meet-
ing, told me that he saw mirror carp, while standing on a bridge
which crosses one of the tributaries of the River Shannon.
I know the bridge myself and it is of no great height, and in
summer the river is usually quite shallow and rather heavily
weeded. I was assured that these fish were carp, weighing perhaps 10 lb., and attempts to drop baits on their noses resulted
in their swimming off.

One explanation which came from official circles was that
they might have been salmon biding their time, but my Birmingham friend, who is an ardent angler, was quite convinced
that they were mirror carp. On another occasion, an angler
visiting a Cavan lough allegedly caught a carp, much to the
surprise of the local angling representatives. The fish was not
preserved, because the angler, understandably, gave little
thought to its capture, but he was quite convinced that the fish
he had caught was of that species. When I heard this report,
my mind immediately went back several years to the time I first
fished that water, for I remembered a visiting angler telling me
that while bream fishing, he had hooked a fish which had sped
towards the centre of the lough and which had eventually
broken his line. I recall that we decided he had hooked a trout,
but we were told that none existed there, and heavy splashes
we had heard after nightfall had been attributed to bream because of this statement. The unverified report of the captured
carp makes the situation most interesting, for it provides an
alternative explanation to the incidents we experienced in late
June 1956.

On another occasion I was fishing a pool in Co. Leitrim and during the early part of the evening I began to hear sucking noises coming from the direction of a bed of lilies. I approached as near as I could to the spot, and although the fish were not visible, the water disturbance caused by their sucking activities was most pronounced. The logical explanation was that I was observing bream feeding on animal life; probably snails eggs laid on the underside of the lily pads. Oddly enough, on first hearing the noises, my mind immediately turned to carp, although it was probably a romantic notion on my part, perhaps partly resulting from the fact that I was fishing a pool on a private estate which could once have been described as being of the ornamental variety. A neatly constructed bank was situated on one side and a copse had been planted nearby, inside which there was a feeling of eerieness as one passed moss-covered rocks in the semi-darkness. Until someone proves otherwise, the above explanation must be the accepted one, but from time to time my mind goes back to the day when a colleague hooked a fish in the pool and I think of the arch formed by the rod as the fish raced off and how the rod straightened out when the line broke some moments later.

As Irish angling progresses, more and more interesting facts about its coarse fish will come to light. Recently, for example, a heavily weeded lough was partly netted and score upon score of specimen tench were caught; 6 lb. fish were plentiful and there were several 7 lb. fish. The carp of the "stew ponds" of Chaucer's England were no doubt conveyed across the Irish Sea, and in more modern and, of course, trout loving Ireland, it is plausible that carp in general became less important as a table commodity and were neglected and ultimately forgotten. Methinks the time is fast approaching when one or two of their descendants are due to be discovered!

IRISH RECORD COARSE FISH

BREAM	11¾ lb.	1882	River Blackwater (Monaghan)	A. Pike
CARP	18 lb. 12 oz.	6/6/1958	Abbey Lake	John Roberts
DACE	1 lb. 2 oz.	8/8/1966	River Blackwater (Cappoquin)	John T. Henry
PERCH	5 lb. 8 oz.	1946	River Erne	S. Drum
PIKE	53 lb.	July 1920	Lough Conn	J. Garvin
ROACH	2 lb. 8 oz.	28/7/1965	River Blackwater (Cappoquin)	Joseph Deane
RUDD	3 lb. 1 oz.	27/6/1959	Kilglass Lake	A. E. Biddlecombe
RUDD/BREAM HYBRID	5 lb. 5 oz.	5/6/1963	Garnafailagh (Coosan Lough)	W. Walker
TENCH	7 lb. 12 oz.	4/6/1966	River Shannon (Nr. Clondra)	Edmund Hawksworth

CONCLUSION

IRELAND CAN OFFER a variety of waters, rarely found elsewhere. Great loughs, small loughs, waters exposed to the four winds and others sheltered and serene; rivers, some wide and far reaching and others temperamental and sometimes frustrating. There are the small rivers and the canals and waters which are neither lough nor river, but a combination of the two, where a maze of islets and weed beds may be found. There are networks of waters so involved that it is difficult to ascertain to which river system they belong, and there are bays on the big loughs, so completely divided by rambling reed beds that they claimed independence long ago from the mother water.

It is to such waters that my various angling friends and I have journeyed on many occasions. It is there that we have learned much about Irish coarse fishing. It is from such waters that we have taken bream as bright as polished pennies or as black as the bogwater in which they live, and pike, desperate in their endeavours to escape gaff or net, and rudd and perch, if not so reluctant, nevertheless not altogether too pleased about having to vacate temporarily their beloved lily pads, gravel runs or shady holts.

"The English Influence" now predominates in Irish coarse fishing, and the sight of a hamper or keep-net is no longer a rare one. Many friendships have been made and wherever one goes, one senses a profound desire on the part of those concerned to further the development of coarse fishing. Perhaps the banks around Carrick-on-Shannon and Portumna and Castleblaney and other angling centres are becoming a little worn, and the occasional weed bed is flattened, but I am obliged to say that the fish have not taken unkindly to the overwhelming attentions bestowed upon them in more recent times.

Gamesmanship, however, or rather a lack of it, has arrived,

but only on the slightest scale. I recall that I have been over-
taken when quite near to a place I was obviously making for,
by others who had decided to drive right up to the water's
edge, while I had decided to walk, and I have been asked to
move from a swim because the person concerned had allegedly
groundbaited it the previous evening. I have also known a fellow angler come to the end of a small stone promontory off
which I was fishing and proceed to cast an artificial lure over
my head. (He very obligingly missed my float as he retrieved
his line.)

These isolated cases have perhaps occurred because those
involved possess that strong will to survive against any odds,
which desire has developed as a result of having to fish over-
populated waters. Certain anglers have been introduced to the
"gentle art" in such an atmosphere, and they do not know how
to act otherwise. A local inhabitant, who was out in his boat,
rowed over my line, pulled up in front of me, and started a
conversation which lasted half an hour or so.

A comparison of the incidents illustrates the ignorance and
selfishness of the former persons and the innocent friendliness
of the latter person. These incidents are centuries apart and one
can only hope that they will remain so.

When one considers that the entire angling population of
England could be accommodated conveniently in Ireland at the
same time, it follows that there is really no need for such unfortunate incidents as aforementioned to arise, and one trusts
that Irish coarse fishing will continue to retain its old world
atmosphere and not be subjected to such happenings to any
material extent.

I have met anglers in Ireland who have been disappointed
with the fishing they have experienced, and on enquiry I have
discovered that they have visited a new situation every day and
commenced fishing from the first stretch of clear bank. They
did not realise that whether a stretch of water is well fished
or never sees a rod from one week to the next, it is necessary
to do more than to assemble one's tackle, bait one's hook and

cast. Other anglers I have met have concentrated their efforts
on one or two well chosen locations and have been more than
satisfied with their catches.

From long experience I have learned never to think too far
ahead about my angling activities in Ireland. There is usually
a wide selection of places to fish at any angling centre, and unless for some specific reason I have a definite prearranged plan
in mind, I prefer to see what sort of weather the day has brought
before venturing out.

Such observations can prevent what would otherwise be
fruitless journeys. I hope that the various comments I have
made on weather conditions in Ireland will be of assistance, for
the subject is an extremely important one and well worthy of
consideration.

When reflecting on the possible future course of Irish angling
one must keep in mind that important organisation, the Inland
Fisheries Trust Incorporated, to which I have previously
referred. The Trust is concerned with the improvement and
development of coarse fishing. It is, in conjunction with the
Irish Government, equally concerned with the growth of brown
trout fishing, but it is in connection with the former subject
that I now wish to illustrate the work which has been under-
taken by this Organisation.

The Trust has made a close survey of many waters in various
parts of Ireland, which are known to contain coarse fish, and in
some instances small loughs, which have been found to hold
undersized perch and rudd, have been cleared of such fish and
tench have taken their place. In certain larger stretches of water,
tench have also been introduced to provide an additional attrac-
tion to pike, perch, bream and rudd. Carp have also been introduced to suitable waters. The Trust also shows a keen interest
and assists in the development of angling centres, and careful
liaison between the Organisation and Angling Clubs and
Associations has resulted in an increase in the amenities available to visiting anglers. Local Angling Committees merit the
highest praise in their own right for the way in which they have

set about the necessary tasks and the strides which have already
been made are both remarkable and commendable.

Of more recent origin is the National Coarse Fishing Federa-
tion of Ireland, of which the Associations of a formidable cross-
section of Irish coarse fishing centres are members, and which
is affiliated to the International Confederation of Anglers
(C.I.P.S.).

Unlike the Inland Fisheries Trust, its aims are primarily
to preserve and develop coarse fishing, as its title suggests,
and also to encourage more anglers to visit Irish centres.

From the foregoing remarks it can be seen that the greatest
efforts are being made at all levels to further the advancement
of Irish coarse fishing and what the position will be in ten years
time is anyone's guess. I do not make this statement rashly
because the whole approach to coarse fishing has changed
dramatically in a few short years, as everyone who has been
connected with the subject will surely agree.

I cannot predict any appreciable lowering of the present
standards. The majority of coarse fish are being returned to the
water by visitors after capture, and one still sees little of hook
and line between November and March. The heavy winter
flooding in many places curtails angling operations and the
number of acres of fishable waters exceeds by far the number of
anglers. There is no cause for concern in this respect and any
shyness or lack of co-operation on the part of the fish, observed
by visiting anglers, could just as eaily be the result of natural
causes or drainage schemes as opposed to over-fishing or the
over-crowding of banks.

The development of tench and carp fishing will undoubtedly
be something to watch with the greatest interest, and perhaps
one or two species of fish beloved by English anglers may be
introduced to certain selected Irish waters. However, no coarse
fish which simulates the fly-taking trout would ever be introduced to any water holding this latter fish and taking the subject as a whole, it might be agreed that the presence of another
bottom feeder would complete the Irish picture. As that most

popular English fish, the roach, is virtually absent from Irish waters and although its close relative the rudd is present in great numbers, the natural habits of this latter fish and the inadequacy of the perch to fully compensate the angler, makes the bream the only widely distributed bottom fish which can bring general satisfaction.

This it does with a consistency and in a manner that will continue to delight for years to come, but it is unfortunate that there is no alternative bottom fish to angle for when bream are absent or in sultry mood. Such an omission has been no detriment to the growth in popularity of the country's fishing, however, but it will be interesting to see if any measures are taken in the future to rectify what "bottom fishermen" might term a defect in Irish angling. The performance of such a task would be an enormous one, but Irish Coarse Fishing has an enormous future and nought will deter the efforts of those in whose hands its future lies.